BIGGER THAN HISTORY

Bigger Than History

Why Archaeology Matters

Brian Fagan

Emeritus Professor, University of California, Santa Barbara

Nadia Durrani

Front cover:
Top: View of Lower Manhattan, New York, USA, at sunset.
Wenjie Dong/Getty Images
Bottom: Angkor Wat, Siem Reap, Cambodia, at dusk.
Martin Puddy/Getty Images

Text by Brian Fagan and Nadia Durrani

Design by Nick Jakins

First published in 2019 in the United States of America by Thames & Hudson Inc., 500 Fifth Avenue, New York, New York 10110

www.thamesandhudsonusa.com

Library of Congress Control Number 2019941933

ISBN 978-0-500-295090

Printed and bound in China by C & C Offset Printing Co. Ltd

To the archaeologists of the future.

> Thus the sum of things is ever being renewed, and mortals live dependent one upon another...and in a short space the generations of living creatures are changed and like runners hand on the torch of life.
>
> Lucretius, *On the Nature of Things*, II, 75.

Contents

Preface

Egyptian pyramids, gold-laden Peruvian tombs, and the lost city of Pompeii: these are some of the great treasures of archaeology. Yet archaeology embraces far more than just the iconic sites. It uncovers all aspects of the human past—from our origins in tropical Africa more than six million years ago to the Industrial Revolution and beyond. We are both archaeologists, and some of our colleagues have investigated the fire of the Woodstock rock festival of 1969, while even the Californian movie set of Cecil B. DeMille's 1923 film *The Ten Commandments* has been ripe for study.

Despite the appeal of Indiana Jones, Lara Croft, or *The Mummy*, we're not wayward adventurers tunneling into pyramids and royal tombs in remote lands with bullwhips and revolvers. The old stereotype of the solitary archaeologist unearthing lost civilizations and pharaonic gold is long dead. Archaeology has become a highly sophisticated way of studying the remote, and not-so-remote, past. Most research involves teamwork, not only in the field, but also in the laboratory. We rely heavily on hi-tech science to tease out minute details of ancient societies and, when preservation conditions allow, of individuals ranging from Egyptian pharaohs and Siberian nomads, to a Bronze Age man from the Alps and mummies from Chile's Atacama Desert. Archaeology is a truly global enterprise.

A global enterprise, but one that some feel is an anachronistic, self-indulgent luxury. They assume that archaeology is stuck in the world of Tutankhamun's tomb and the attempts to make astonishing discoveries, an academic pastime that flourishes in an ivory tower. From there, it's a short step to labeling it irrelevant and unnecessary in today's fast-changing world. This is absolute nonsense, for archaeology brings the entire human past to life, and gives us much greater insight into ourselves as a species—revealing our similarities or differences—and how we came to be who we are today.

Of course, one cannot use the past as a way of forecasting the future, but unearthing information about our forebears is invaluable to gaining a better understanding of ourselves. After all, "The contemporary world is a product of the past," as Rosemary Joyce remarked in 2008.

We have an enormous amount to learn from the past, which makes archaeology of profound importance to the present. In the following chapters, we hope to show you why. We'll explore how archaeology is far more than excavations, surveys, and museum artifacts. We will start with the big issue of climate change, and show how archaeology is providing unique perspectives on how our forebears adapted to such change. We shall send a challenge to the climate-change deniers, who say that the earth has faced these challenges before. From climate change, we delve into human social changes over time, starting with identity. First, we tackle race and ethnicity, uncovering information that rewrites what many assumed they knew about their identity based on appearance or their supposed origins. Then we'll turn to those groups without written history, among them the poor, women, and children—all of whom find their places in the dirt of the past. From there, we move to gender, offering cross-cultural case studies that provide valuable ammunition in today's debates on gender identity. In Chapter 5, we show how archaeology has become enmeshed in political and nationalistic agendas. Current archaeological thinking has moved far beyond the simplistic theories of cultists to serious explorations of the relationships between oral traditions, indigenous histories, and archaeology. Such research often involves local communities, with archaeologists combining their work with indigenous perspectives to reconstruct a past for the benefit of the locals, as among the Maya people of Chocolá, Guatemala. Here, and throughout this book, we will see how one of the greatest values of archaeology is that it is as much about the anonymous many as it is about the elite few.

Today's archaeologists confront many challenges. Our work is undergoing a major sea change, as the priceless records of the past vanish in the face of industrial development and population growth. The crisis of site destruction and looting has deepened, to the point that there are fewer and fewer undisturbed locations each year. While this happens, more and more archaeology now unfolds in the laboratory, as the focus changes from solely discovery to conservation of the fragile archives of the past also, which are melting like snow. Conservation and protection of the past go hand in hand with another reality—that preserving the cultural heritage of humanity, be it spectacular pyramids or just a scatter of stone tools, for future generations is the greatest priority of all. Without a past, we lack context and precedent, the chance to learn from the experiences of our forebears. Rapidly increasing cultural tourism, deep agriculture, road construction, and expanding cities are also devastating the record of the past. Add to this the crowding at major sites, such as Egypt's Valley of the Kings, or at Altamira, or Pompeii, and we have the ironic situation that we are loving the past to death and unwittingly destroying it. We look closely at these issues in later chapters.

New challenges, a crisis for the past, and new priorities: to cope, the archaeology of tomorrow will have to be very different from that of today, which values discovery over anything else. We lay out some of the trends and the need for urgent change in the ways archaeologists go about their business. Above all, we argue passionately that archeology has a vital role to play in today's industrialized world. It is the study of us and our experience over millions of years, and understanding one another is, after all, one of the most urgent challenges facing humanity.

Acknowledgments

Mark Sapwell of Thames & Hudson asked us to write this book and encouraged us from the beginning. We're very grateful for his guidance, and that of his colleagues Ben Hayes and George Maudsley. Shelly Lowenkopf was, as always, an invaluable adviser. We're grateful to the many colleagues who have helped us, and critiqued our work over the years. Their insights were a major factor in the writing of these pages.

Brian Fagan
Santa Barbara, California

Nadia Durrani
London, England

		YEARS BEFORE PRESENT	EVENT
ARCHAEOLOGY	HISTORY	Today	The computer age; global capitalism
		250	Dawn of the Industrial Revolution; emergence of nation states
		500	European colonial expansion ("the Age of Discovery")
		2,000	Imperial Rome brings written records to northern Europe
		3,000–2,000	Diverse writing systems develop, including in China and Mexico
		3,000	Oldest alphabet in Phoenicia, eastern Mediterranean
		5,000	Cuneiform script in Mesopotamia; hieroglyphic script in Egypt
	PREHISTORY	12,000	"Neolithic Revolution": agriculture, settled life in Middle East; Ice Age ends
		15,000	First settlement of the Americas
		40,000	*Homo sapiens* in Europe
		65,000	*Homo sapiens* in Asia and Oceania
		120,000	*Homo sapiens* become fully anatomically modern
		300,000	*Homo sapiens* (emerge in Africa)
		400,000	Neanderthals (emerge in Eurasia)
		1.9 million	*Homo ergaster/erectus* (outside of Africa *c.* 1.8 million years ago)
		3.3 million	Oldest known human-made stone tools
		4.2 million	Australopithecines emerge
		7 million	Human ("hominin") lineage splits from that of the chimpanzees in Africa

All dates are approximate. New discoveries constantly impact these dates, particularly those far back in time.

Bigger than history: if we imagine the span of human existence in terms of a twenty-four-hour clock, with our earliest ancestors (around 6 million years ago) emerging at midnight, then the first of our species, *Homo sapiens* (dated to around 300,000 years ago) would have turned up at around 22.48, the first farmers (around 10,000 years ago) at 23.57 and 36 seconds, while the first written historical records (5,000 years ago) come in at 23.58 and 48 seconds. Archaeology covers this entire span, while history explores the last minute or so of human existence.

1 Revealing Deep History

Why does archaeology matter? Why should we spend precious resources on the study of the human past? What possible benefit is archaeology to society? This book is about tackling these questions. While a steady stream of television documentaries, newspaper stories, and websites bombard us with the sensational discoveries of archaeology, many people have no idea of what most archaeologists do, or of the subject's value to society. There is still a widespread impression that archaeology is a luxurious endeavor or a frivolous hobby, of no benefit to society at a time when there is a global poverty crisis, a growing gap between rich and poor, and a host of environmental challenges.

Archaeologists aim to study, conserve, and interpret all aspects of our human past, the results of which can help us face these challenges. Such an enterprise is driven by the idea that one cannot fully understand the present, or attempt to look to the future, without a knowledge of what went before. "Study the past if you would define the future," asserted Confucius 2500 years ago. "Those who fail to learn from history are doomed to repeat it," noted Churchill in 1948. "You have to know the past to understand the present," said astrophysicist Carl Sagan in 1980.

Unfortunately, the notion of archaeology as a luxury pursuit even permeates the lofty heights of college and university education. It is often high on the list of programs to be cut on the grounds that it is non-essential, does not bring in large grants, and is not a way to guarantee employment for graduates. Yet this ignores the fact that the study of archaeology produces informed people capable of making rational decisions about such fundamental issues as climate change, diversity and equality, governance, and sustainability—just a few of the areas dealt with by archaeology today.

Yes, the past is another world but, as we will show, a knowledge of the past illuminates the dimensions of often challenging issues and decisions in the present. It lets us examine ourselves over a long-term perspective, on a global scale, with all the cultural continuity and change that this entails. This in turn allows us to question modern behavior—particularly when justifications for attitudes on particular issues are assumed to have ancient or natural origins, as is the case for such ideas as racial differences, ethnic or national identities, economic or sexual inequality, or the ways we ought to express our gender. In all of these areas, which we will discuss, archaeology certainly has something to say. And more often than not, the conversation has far-reaching implications.

Bigger than History

Tutankhamun was an obscure Egyptian pharaoh, who died young in 1323 BC, and was buried hastily in a richly adorned tomb. Ironically, this little-known, short-lived ruler became world-famous after Howard Carter and Lord Carnarvon discovered his undisturbed sepulcher in 1922. The opening of the tomb caused a global sensation, as did the excavations of the royal burials at Ur in southern Iraq by Leonard Woolley four years later, and those of the Anglo-Saxon Sutton Hoo ship burial in the UK in the late 1930s. These, and other spectacular finds before World War II, captured public imagination and showed how archaeology was able to reveal important information about otherwise forgotten people and their worlds. Yet an archaeologist of the 1930s would be amazed by today's practitioners. We now rely heavily on high-technology science and on researchers from all kinds of academic disciplines, from biology, genetics, and geology to physics and zoology, to mention only a few. The complex combination of techniques and disciplines that make up archaeology masks its unique role in today's world.

The most distinctive quality of archaeology is the timescale with which it deals. Archaeologists think in millennia, in hundreds of thousands of years, and only rarely in centuries or smaller units of time. By contrast, historians—who work primarily with written and documentary sources—

tend to focus on a given century, year, or even day, hour, or minute. And since historians rely on written sources, they do not study prehistory—the great span of time before writing—nor do they study places or people for whom no written or oral records exist. Archaeology is never limited to the words of literate people, by geography, or time.

We explore all physical remains related to past human behavior. Reaching into the far past, archaeology is therefore sometimes called "deep history." Our archives include anything humans left behind, including tools, food remains (whether animal bones or plant remains), human skeletal remains, inscriptions and other written records, art, temples, and the total detritus of deserted human settlements. Many years ago, an eminent British archaeologist, Stuart Piggott, memorably called archaeology "the science of rubbish." But it's far more. We alone among all students of humanity study human biological and cultural change over the entire stretch of human existence.

The greatest developments in archaeology have come since the 1960s, with a growing reliance on a variety of scientific approaches. Within academia, this has resulted in a much more specialized archaeology, with subfields ranging from Assyriology to ethnoarchaeology, paleoanthropology, underwater archaeology, and zooarchaeology. This research, while often crucially important, can be obscure, esoteric stuff, effectively impenetrable to the wider public. Indeed, as with all scholarly disciplines, academic archaeology is often swamped by jargon and theory, much of which is fully intelligible to only a handful of acolytes.

In many countries, however, including the USA and UK, academic archaeology exists alongside a second major strand of archaeology: developer-funded work. The latter goes by various names, including commercial archaeology (UK), or cultural resource management (USA). Unlike university research-led projects, which can take years of fine-grained study, such projects usually have a strict timescale ahead of the building or mining work. Commercial archaeologists usually aim to record (or preserve) as much of the archaeology as possible ahead of its potential destruction by development. These are different pressures, but carry the same intention: to record and understand the past.

In both cases, whether academic or commercial, archaeology is threatened with funding cuts and competing priorities, and no archaeologist, whatever his or her background, can work in an ivory tower cut off from the contemporary world. This is a powerful reality, requiring changes in the ways in which today's archaeologists go about their business. More than ever, archaeologists strive to make their work relevant to the modern world: questions of human migration, social inequality, or environmental sustainability are just a few of our concerns today. So, too, is the preservation of the global cultural heritage of humankind for future generations. Are these new directions in archaeology a good thing? Most emphatically, yes. After more than a century and a half of formal discovery and excavation, we have now uncovered enough to make credible attempts to put our understanding of the past into practice, and to undertake the daunting responsibilities of preserving it.

The chapters that follow describe some of the big issues that archaeologists confront. At this juncture, it is therefore vital to give you an impression of the broad scope of deep history, as this is, after all, archaeology's primary objective. Let us briefly explore some of the major developments of the past studied by archaeologists, all of which we will discuss further in the rest of the book.

Human Origins

We begin with the question of questions. How old are our remotest ancestors? Were they created on 23 October 4004 BC as the Irish bishop James Ussher famously calculated from Old Testament genealogies in AD 1650? Or a more formidable 25,000 years old, 100,000, or even older? Enter Louis and Mary Leakey, who had long searched for human ancestors at Olduvai Gorge on Tanzania's Serengeti Plain. In 1959, they unearthed the large and heavy skull of a hominin (a term used to describe modern humans, and extinct human species) they named *Zinjanthropus boisei*, or, as Mary called it, "Dear Boy" (see Figure 1). It lay among fragmentary animal bones, and crude stone flakes and jagged-edged chopping tools by a shallow lake. A new geological dating method, potassium argon dating, told the Leakeys that *Zinjanthropus* was a staggering 1.75 million years old.

This was just the beginning. The Leakeys' find, and their subsequent discoveries at Olduvai, unleashed a torrent of new research involving not only archaeologists but also multidisciplinary research teams, working on the shores of Lake Turkana in northern Kenya, in desolate landscapes in Ethiopia, and in South Africa. Thus was born paleoanthropology, the study

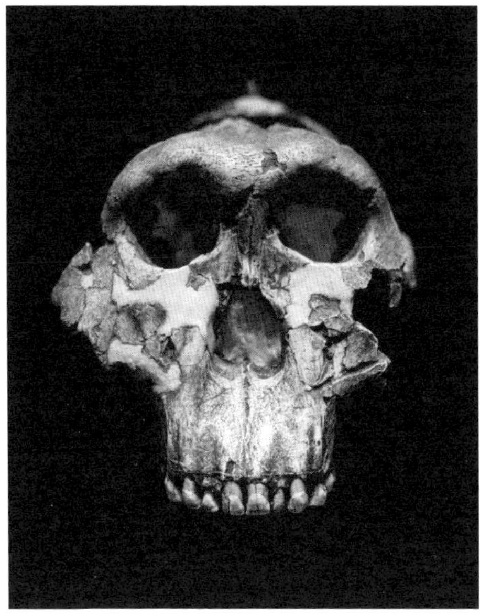

Figure 1. ***Zinjanthropus boisei*** **from Olduvai Gorge, Tanzania, dating to c. 1.75 million years ago.** Found by Mary Leakey in 1959.

of early human evolution and behavior, which involves specialisms of all kinds—not only archaeology, but biological anthropology, human genetics, and geology, too.

We now know that our human (or hominin) lineage split from that of the chimpanzees around 7 million years ago, while the earliest traces of human cultural behavior, defined by the making of crude stone tools, currently date to 3.33 million years ago. It is unclear precisely which hominin made these first tools, and their makers might not even have been our direct ancestors. Far from being a neat ladder, human evolutionary models look more like a series of disjointed brush strokes. To date, researchers have identified more than twenty ancient hominin species. The relationships between the various forms, however, are often unclear and thus contested, with several species coexisting at any given time, and some dying out without giving rise to later species.

So who are we now and how do we fit into the evolutionary picture? We are *Homo sapiens*, the self-named "wise people": creatures endowed with advanced cognitive abilities—fluent speech, the ability to innovate, plan, and think ahead. These abilities may have been shared by other contemporary hominins, such as our Neanderthal cousins (who lived between about 400,000 to perhaps 30,000 years ago). Yet *Homo sapiens* took things further, transforming the world in unparalleled ways.

Africa is our homeland, and the oldest known examples of our species date to more than 300,000 years ago. Yet the earliest specimens are not quite fully anatomically modern, something that seems to have occurred around 120,000 years ago. Controversy surrounds what happened next and our subsequent movements out of Africa. The Qafzeh Cave in Israel has evidence for the existence of fully anatomically modern humans—that is, people whose skeletons are just like ours, and presumably with the same mental potential as any of us—around 120,000 to 80,000 years ago. A solitary 84,000-year-old modern toe bone comes from the Saudi Arabian desert, from an area that was better watered than today. From radiocarbon dates and other dating methods, we know that modern humans were in Europe by 40,000 years ago, and in Australia even earlier. Dozens of archaeologists and research teams are searching for the earliest modern humans from the eastern Mediterranean to the Cape of Good Hope, deep into China, south and southeast Asia, and northeastern Siberia, and in the Americas as well, where people settled at least 15,000 years ago. After some 7 million years of human evolution, *Homo sapiens* is the only hominin left standing, and we are the focus of most archaeological endeavors, and of this book.

Getting Domesticated

As the subsequent millennia unfolded, our nomadic hunter-gatherer ancestors began to move slowly across the globe. The rate of cultural change started to quicken. For the first time in hominin history, the late Ice Age (*c.* 30,000 to 12,000 years ago) saw bursts of extreme artistic creativity, exemplified by the exquisite rock art of southwestern Europe and western Eurasia. Although it's easy to feel a profound human connection with these early artists, the late Ice Age world was unimaginably different to that of today.

Global sea levels were 300 feet (90 meters) below modern levels, Siberia and Alaska were connected, and Britain was part of the European continent because the North Sea was dry land. As ice sheets melted and the world warmed, sea levels rose and forest vegetation spread northward across

Europe and North America with the increase in temperature. Late Ice Age hunters adapted to a more environmentally diverse world where warmer and cooler temperatures fluctuated in irregular cycles. But at about 12,900 years ago, a thousand-year cold snap settled over northern latitudes of the world. The near-arctic temperatures brought arid conditions across Europe, as they often had during the late Ice Age, and triggered an extensive drought in southwestern Asia. Hunting populations there were forced to cluster near permanent water sources, but the drought was one of a number of major factors that influenced the development of a new form of subsistence: animal husbandry and agriculture—what today we call food production. Water shortages, and scarce grazing lands and plant foods, brought wild herd animals and humans into much closer association. Human societies clustered at close quarters and thus became more anchored to the territories they were now inhabiting.

Agriculture and animal farming may seem mundane to some, but food production was one of the great catalysts of human history. Few other cultural developments can be considered to be of greater importance. It meant a regular source of food and, in many cases, led to population booms: villages swelled, and farmers looking for more space migrated across continents, replacing or merging with native hunting communities. Agriculture also meant that, once invested in a crop, people were for the first time tied to their land all year round, leading to new forms of social organization, and raising complex questions about inheritance, kin ties, and access to food surplus and wealth. In some parts of the world, intensive agriculture did not lead to population booms, but eventually brought about environmental changes that forced populations to migrate or perish. Animal husbandry meant that people lived in close association with their animals. Their lives were closely interconnected with their herds, especially in environments with frequent droughts, when people relied on kin living in better-watered areas to look after their herds. For humans, living in the first, crowded, villages meant that infectious diseases spread readily. As did such conditions as dysentery, caused by contaminated water supplies. Agriculture and animal husbandry constituted a two-edged sword, but an unprecedented engine for change.

Food production is known to us from subtle archaeological clues—changes in wild grasses that became the wheat, maize, and rice of today; from DNA and minute anatomical differences in the bones of wild and domestic cattle, goats, and sheep caused by captive breeding; and major changes in human settlements. With this evidence, archaeologists still ask many questions about the origins of agriculture. What social and economic changes resulted? Was the shift from hunting to agriculture a ready transition, or did some societies switch back and forth between, say, cattle herding and hunting? The changeover, it seems, was sometimes rapid, but often occurred gradually over many centuries—even millennia; yet, in the end, food production became the dominant means of subsistence. But the ultimate, and fundamental, question of great relevance today is how did farmers address the complex issue of sustainability?

Complicated, and still little understood, factors played a role in this dramatic economic shift, which took hold independently in widely separated hunter-gatherer societies throughout the Old World and the Americas. Potatoes were cultivated in the Andes as early as 10,000 years ago, maize and beans in Central America somewhat later. We know that the new economies spread like wildfire in some regions—from the Near East into Europe by 6000 BC, into the Nile Valley at about the same time. The same was true wherever farming took hold. Within a few millennia, many small settlements in all regions became ever-larger villages, then towns. Town populations could number in the lower thousands. By 4000 BC, many much more complex towns were becoming what archaeologists loosely define as cities, with populations of 10,000 or more in the Near East; less than a millennium later, some of these cities became the first large urban centers, emerging between the Tigris and Euphrates rivers in Iraq, and along the Nile.

Building Cities

After 3000 BC, the compass of human existence widened beyond the confines of villages and towns. As populations grew, some people began to live in ever-larger and more complex settlements, which archaeologists define as "cities." The size of the city varied, but populations were still low compared to today—in 2000 BC, Ur in Mesopotamia was the largest city in the world, with an estimated population of 65,000. How cities functioned and looked also varied depending on time and place, but most were divided into different zones (rich, poor, industrial, and so on), and usually contained public buildings; they had written records, and their inhabitants produced works of art. They tended to be dominated by a ruling class or religious authority, and their people usually engaged in wide-ranging trading, strengthening or initiating political and social relationships with distant communities.

In many cases, cities depended for much of their lifeblood on long-distance trade and exchange. Imagine a square-sailed river boat carrying grain from the fertile Nile delta to the temple of the sun god Amun at Waset (now Luxor); a small caravan of donkeys carrying bundles of textiles from the River Tigris deep into Turkey; or llamas carrying sacred mollusks along mountain paths in the Andes. With the rise of civilization came a much more interconnected world: the Sumerians and Babylonians of the Near East traded far and wide, engaging in a major third millennium BC trade route between "Meluhha" (the Indus Valley of today's Pakistan) and the Arabian Peninsula. By 1200 BC their network encompassed the entire eastern Mediterranean. These links are evident in a remarkable cargo aboard a heavily laden merchant vessel wrecked on the rocks of Uluburun in southern Turkey in 1305 BC (see Plate 1). Its cargo came from nine different areas, including ebony wood from the Nile, and enough copper ingots to equip a regiment from Cyprus.

The trajectory of deep history includes the people of the Indus Valley, Mesopotamia and Egypt, the Chinese dynasties, the Persians, the Mycenaeans, the Greeks, the Maya, and those of many other societies. For those whose scripts we can read, we know the names and dates of their rulers, and sometimes much about their achievements. Yet one of archaeology's key values is its ability to explore beyond the written accounts that were so often about, or by, the elite few. We range beyond palaces, or kings and queens, to look for signs of the anonymous—farmers, fishers, weavers, tillers, the ill, the poor, the miscreants, and the marginalized. Many new techniques are helping to improve our knowledge of everyday people in the past. One of the most exciting is laser imagery, known as Light Detection and Ranging (LiDAR), which has the ability to pierce the thick rainforests and reveal the hidden ruins beneath. LiDAR has exposed the intricate hinterlands of great Maya centers and the magnificent Khmer temple at Angkor Wat in Cambodia. For a long time archaeologists thought that such great city centers were isolated and self-sustaining, dominated by extensive temple complexes. Thanks to LiDAR, we now have maps of entire neighborhoods and elaborate water-management systems that surrounded the ceremonial precincts over an area of 6.6 square miles (17 square kilometers) or more. For the first time, the surrounding forests have been removed electronically, so we can peer through the dense forest cover to what lies beneath. LiDAR scanning revealed that Maya cities were in fact interconnected by networks of wide, elevated causeways, peppered with smaller communities and hamlets. More than 60,000 Maya structures—among them houses, fortifications, and causeways—have been found in Guatemala so far. These discoveries have exploded previous estimates of the size of the Maya population, and given us a better sense of the ordinary people living around the famous Maya temples.

Archaeology has also shed light on other anonymous groups: Viking settlers in Greenland, colonists in Jamestown, Virginia, and those living in small farming villages in East Africa. It adds new dimensions to the understanding of ancient pueblo societies in the American Southwest, uncovers the strategy behind 8,000-year-old bison hunts on the Great Plains, or details of an eighteenth-century Maori earthwork in New Zealand. Archaeology has a scope that extends from simple hominin stopping-places in East Africa's Rift Valley to a pickle factory in Victorian London. No other form of historical inquiry can, for example, tunnel into the base of Maya pyramids and use deciphered glyphs to reconstruct their architectural history. Archaeologists study the history of everyone and provide a unique, broad understanding of the past.

Today's archaeology is detail obsessed, but this obsession is often necessary in order to record accurately the details of past cultures. Archaeologists strive to document the past as scientifically and meticulously as possible: we dig according to careful protocol, and we scrutinize the data using scientific methods, including carbon-14 dating and DNA analysis. The results can mean that accepted historical facts are overturned, which is perhaps not so surprising when we remember that much of history was written (and therefore embellished) by the victors and the elite. Indeed, time and again, archaeology provides a far more complete, and potentially more objective, picture than if we relied solely on historical written or oral accounts. In addition, while archaeology has its famous sparkling treasures, we've seen how it works to reveal the whole human experience in its sometimes unglamorous detail, and to include all our ancestors from every corner of the world. It is a vital step to understanding others and, through them, ourselves.

What makes us human? How are you and I different or similar? How did we do things in the past? What lessons can be learned from the past? How can we use the past to improve our present, or even our future? It is this wide perspective of our deep history that archaeology brings to bear on the issues of today.

Figure 2. An artist's reconstruction of a hunter-gatherer camp in the heart of Doggerland, now the North Sea, *c.* 7000 BC. Hundreds of small hunting and fishing bands had to move frequently to higher ground in the face of rising sea levels.

2 Investigating Climate Change

Apprehension, denial, fear, and careful preparation: these are qualities that surround modern debates about climatic shifts in an era of sustained global warming. Did humans, through industrial pollution and greenhouse emissions, cause the rapidly increasing global temperatures of the past century and a half? Or is the current warming simply part of the long-term natural cycles of the earth's ever-oscillating climate?

Scientific consensus embraces the former stance, holding that current global warming is almost certainly the result of human behavior, particularly the practice of fossil-fuel combustion. "It is extremely likely," stated the Intergovernmental Panel on Climate Change in 2013, "that human influence has been the dominant cause of the observed warming since the mid-twentieth century." No formal opinion of any scientific body dissents from this assessment. Yet pitted against the rigorous research of the scientific community are the climate-change deniers. Speaking in 2003, US Senator James Inhofe dismissed all climate-change research as "phony science," further speculating whether "man-made global warming is the greatest hoax ever perpetrated on the American people." In 2017, US Senator John Barrasso said, "The climate is constantly changing. The role human activity plays is not known." Both men, however, are known supporters of the oil and gas industries. There is a sustained campaign of misinformation being put in front of the American public, and probably those of other countries, too. Alas, it has been somewhat successful, but the success will not endure. The partisan debate will doubtless continue, but in the meantime, we cannot ignore that we are living in a warming world. We do not know exactly what climatic change will bring, but archaeology can add to the conversation.

So, what can it teach us? By exploring the impact of human activity on the environment—and over a huge time span—archaeology can highlight the myriad ways in which our ancestors adapted to the challenges of some major past climatic shifts. As we face a future that is set to include increasingly extreme weather, prolonged droughts, and rising sea levels, the past provides a sobering background.

Much of what we know about past climate change is thanks to a revolution in the study of ancient climate change since the late 1970s. Climatic curves derived from the study of deep-sea cores and from deep borings into Arctic and Antarctic glaciers tell us that the past two million years have witnessed at least nine, sometimes intense, glacial periods, interspersed by warmer intervals, known as interglacials, when global temperatures were close to, or even higher, than today's. In other words, humans have experienced global warming—and cooling—several times already. The details come into closer focus with the last glacial period, which began about 100,000 years ago and ended with rapid, if irregular, warming around 12,000 years before present. The coldest millennia of the last glaciation descended on northern latitudes about 18,000 years ago, leaving vast glaciers in Scandinavia and the Alps and much of North America mantled in huge ice sheets; treeless steppe and tundra extended from the Atlantic into Siberia.

There are all kinds of climatic shifts that have impacted people in the past. Some were long-term changes, like the swings between glacials and interglacials, which spanned tens of thousands of years. Shorter changes were commonplace as well, such as a thousand-year-long cold event called the Younger Dryas that brought near-glacial conditions back to Europe and North America around 12,900 years ago and caused a catastrophic drought to descend over parts of Asia. While the archaeology consistently demonstrates how these brief fluctuations affected human societies in multiple ways, it is the long- and short-term economic, political, and social impacts that result from them that are important to discern and understand. Archaeology gives us many examples of where humans have responded and adapted to climatic and environmental changes, and these histories offer us guidance in how to approach the challenges we face today.

After the Ice

Around 15,000 years ago, global sea levels were roughly 300 feet (90 meters) below modern levels. The North Sea was dry land; a huge river estuary flowed through the English Channel; Siberia and Alaska were one; and chains of close islands enabled settlers from Southeast Asia to migrate into Australia. But before long, the ice would begin to melt and the world's landscape would change radically.

Thanks to sophisticated geophysical data, we know that, as early as 12,000 years ago, the once dry land that linked Britain to Europe began to be inundated by the thawing ice. By 7,500 years ago, this wide land bridge had been entirely flooded by what is today's North Sea. Isolated harpoon points and other tools document a post-Ice Age human presence along its low-lying waterways and wetlands. This world, now deep underwater, is named Doggerland, after the Dogger Bank, which is today a large sandbank in a shallow area of the North Sea around 62 miles (100 kilometers) off the east coast of England.

Those who inhabited post-Ice Age Doggerland lived amid a dynamic landscape. Inexorably rising sea levels must have had a visible impact on familiar terrain within a generation, the topography being much reduced, and water level rises measurable in multiple centimeters a year. In this increasingly watery environment, the Doggerlanders must have spent most of their lives afloat in canoes. But, since they belonged to small nomadic groups, they could move effortlessly, and at short notice, to higher ground and new hunting and fishing territories (see Figure 2). There was the space to do so in a relatively sparsely populated landscape. For thousands of years after the Ice Age, people's vulnerability to climate change was therefore minimal.

However, something happened after the ice melted. With the warming temperatures of the Holocene geological epoch, a new era of human economy began—which we call the Neolithic. During the Neolithic, people settled down and farmed. The reasons for this are many, complex, and much debated, but while the Neolithic used to be thought of as a wonderful revolution, this new way of living was not necessarily always so easy.

Anthropologists working with modern hunter-gatherers (that is, people who are not farmers and have not settled down) have observed that they tend to get more rest and expend fewer calories obtaining food when compared to farmers. Moreover, the problem with a settled lifestyle is that once people invested in the land, they became at risk from environmental change. When villagers began to build homes, grow crops, and clear land for animals, it meant they were now (seasonally or year round) anchored to the land and local water supplies.

Unlike the Doggerlanders in their canoes, many of the first farmers would have been unwilling or unable to move at short notice. Instead, they would be forced to find new ways of dealing with sometimes major environmental change, or else they starved. Some of these issues were natural, but others were caused by the very economy they were now pursuing. The Neolithic witnessed previously unseen human-caused land erosion and soil depletion. Furthermore, population numbers began to rise—again the reasons are many, but in a vicious circle, human population growth appears to be linked to a more abundant food supply, which in turn requires bigger families (more children) to farm the land and manage animals. Today, there are almost eight billion of us on the planet. The economy our ancestors set in motion in the Neolithic continues, and has intensified. In looking back over the millennia, particularly those from the Neolithic on, people's responses to environmental change—whether natural or caused by our hands—provide interesting lessons for the future, as this chapter will reveal.

Adapting to Change

Today, we tend to think of climate change in sweeping global terms. But a big lesson from the past is that we find a huge number of adaptations to the problems that beset people, which were, as today, specific to the region or even to a given site. Climate shifts could last one rainy season, bring sudden floods, and wash away crops grown on less fertile land. Droughts might endure for generations, arrive and depart in unpredictable cycles, or affect a farming or herding community but leave another untouched only a few miles away. Sometimes, groups thrived in the face of great challenges. Such cases offer guidance in our own diverse and unpredictable world.

For example, the well-organized Indus Valley civilization, centered in what is now modern-day Pakistan, flourished between 3000 and 1300 BC, despite enduring some dramatic climate change. Between c. 2500 and 1900 BC, the monsoons became less predictable and the rainfall far weaker than a few hundred years before. For many great urban centers this would have spelled doom, yet the Indus civilization continued for another five hundred years. But how?

It used to be argued that climate change forced the people of the Indus to intensify or diversify their farming, but more recent research undertaken by Petrie Cameron at Cambridge University has shown how people were already farming highly varied crops, making them well adapted to variable environmental conditions long before serious climate change set in, and before they even built their first cities. Because they avoided vast monocultures (cultivating only a single crop), they weren't dependent on a particular crop that might then fail with a poor monsoon. As modern agriculturalists make decisions on whether to expand their monocultures, or invest in a more diverse range of crops, the answer from the ancient Indus Valley farmers is clear: diversify where possible.

Yet diversification is not always possible for today's farmers who are faced with demands for ever-cheaper food for a growing population. Intensive monoculture farming, however, means that natural resources risk depletion, if not irrevocable damage. Industrial chemicals, pesticides, and antibiotics may have transformed production levels, but they can be expensive to the environment, as well as to human and animal health. Yet sometimes archaeology reveals forgotten techniques that are both more productive and less damaging than current farming methods.

Working around Bolivia's Lake Titicaca, a team led by Clark Erickson of the University of Penn discovered 202,600 acres (82,000 hectares) of ancient raised fields, made up of high soil beds that were fed by the lake's wetlands. In a five-year experiment, the archaeologists used this ancient raised field method to grow potatoes. The result: more than twice the amount of potatoes per acre compared with the yield of regular fields. An added bonus was that the raised fields could also be used year-round, since they were fertilized by the lake water. The long-term effects and underlying causes of this ancient method are still being analyzed, but this case study offers some interesting food for thought.

Likewise, in south-west Arabia (modern Yemen), over thousands of years, farmers developed various sophisticated methods of agriculture and irrigation. Perhaps most famous are the terraced fields of the central highlands (see Plate 2). The terraces are small cut platforms that tier down entire hillsides upon which crops would be grown. They work by cleverly harnessing the seasonal *seil*, or flash flood, rainfall so that each platform field is well watered. Strict rules ensured the water was fairly diverted to all terraces, each of which was usually owned and worked by a given family. Archaeologists have dated the earliest terraces to around 5000 years ago, but despite their ancient heritage, a significant number have fallen into disrepair in recent decades. Warfare, grinding poverty, and unprecedented migration into the cities by the workforce of young men mean that entire mountainside systems have been negatively impacted. The highlands are a lush and bountiful area, but difficult to reach and farm with mechanical industrial instruments. It seems that the old terrace systems really are the most effective way of farming them.

Today, dealing with climate change seems like an enormous challenge. Many of us feel powerless, believing that what we do as individuals makes little difference. Yet, as with the above examples, what people do at a local level is exactly what matters. Many governments across the world are appreciating the importance of adapting to and mitigating climate change locally. Likewise, climate researchers are focusing in on the community level. In various African countries, such as Burkina Faso, Mozambique, and Zambia, subsistence farmers are having to adapt and adjust to drier and warmer conditions. Issues of food security are being addressed by the African Forest Landscape Restoration Initiative, which aims to restore 247 million acres (100 million hectares) of degraded land by 2030. So far, twenty-one African countries are involved, and farmers are being given technical and financial support to address local issues. In Kenya, for example, work is concentrated on reforestation, wildlife issues, and also on agroforestry, whereby farmers grow trees and shrubs among or around crops to reduce erosion and increase biodiversity. By funding local changes, the Initiative intends to enable great change across a vast area of the continent.

Community Ties

In the Indus Valley, we have seen how people improved their resilience to climate change by diversifying their agriculture, so that a failing crop could be supported by another. Archaeology demonstrates that another major way humans have defended themselves against local climate change is by forming solid relationships across regions, usually sanctified by ideas of marriage, blood, law, ritual, the gods—or all of these. Powerful obligations and rules link such social groups. Anthropologists call these ties "reciprocal relationships": the assumption that others will help you when needed, just as you will help them. The more demanding the environment, often the more important such relationships are. In many societies, reciprocal kin ties, no matter if they live near or far, dominate everyday life. Cattle-herding groups in the Sahel region immediately south of the Sahara Desert protect themselves from drought and shortages of grazing by breeding as many cattle as possible while the rains are good, on the assumption that numbers will give them a measure of security. They also disperse their herds to relatives living near and far. Farmers confronted with drought and highly localized rainfall turn to kin living sometimes only a short distance away, where the rains have been better, to obtain seed and to feed themselves. Such obligations, which are coded into oral traditions, ritual, and respect for ancestors, were routine in most subsistence farming societies. Chaco Canyon in New Mexico offers a powerful example of the effects of close, enduring social ties in the midst of climate change.

Chaco Canyon, in the heart of New Mexico's San Juan Basin, is famous for its spectacular multistory pueblos, which flourished in the heart of an unpredictable, semi-arid landscape. The ancestral Pueblo communities that lived at Chaco flourished between about AD 800 (or earlier) and 1300. The canyon itself is a flat valley bounded by steep cliffs that the twisting Chaco Wash passes through like a serpent. The inhabitants of the canyon used water from the Chaco Wash and from cliff seeps to cultivate its arid soils. In this dry environment, we find not only small villages, but also examples of large pueblos, much bigger structures commonly known as "Great Houses," scattered through the canyon. The largest and most famous of these is Pueblo Bonito (see Figure 3), a semicircular structure with four stories and about 700 rooms, constructed from sandstone blocks and veneered masonry, and strengthened with interior cores of boulders, as well as numerous timber beams. In its heyday, this enormous and imposing pueblo covered at least 3 acres (1.2 hectares), its rooms including living spaces, storage areas, and also subterranean *kivas*—ritual chambers used in ceremonies of all kinds. Pueblo Bonito lay on a north–south axis and was an intensely sacred place—the arms of the semicircle of rooms wrapped around great underground *kivas*, a major focus of ceremonial activity, especially at the solstices.

Smaller pueblos and villages lay throughout the canyon. Chaco Canyon was a place that supported an estimated 2,200 people via carefully managed irrigation agriculture, a testimony to the Chacoan's skills at food production

Figure 3. Pueblo Bonito: a Chaco Canyon "Great House." The large circles in the open plazas are subterranean *kivas*, once roofed over, and used for ritual observances.

under highly unpredictable conditions. Environmental information from Chaco Canyon shows how the region experienced only sporadic rain. What water fell was carefully controlled from run-offs from the bedrock, and collected in canals and dams.

At times, the population of the canyon swelled, as people from the surrounding basin congregated at Chaco. Human existence depended on the performance of elaborate rituals that brought together farmers living over hundreds of square miles of arid landscapes. We know of these long-distance ties because distinctive pottery forms and trade goods can be traced at site after site lying significant distances from the canyon. These regions were connected by still little understood "roads" that spanned hundreds of miles. Chaco Canyon was undoubtedly an intensely sacred place, a ritual magnet for communities living far away, part of a Pueblo world that depended heavily on social ties carefully nurtured across long distances.

The Great Houses depended on food raised in a semi-arid landscape where water supplies were, at best, unreliable. Thanks to precise tree-ring sequences (dendrochronology) derived from dozens of trees and pueblo beams, we can track the savage drought cycles that plagued Chaco during the twelfth century. Maize yields, one of the main staples at Chaco, fell catastrophically after 1130. By this time, the people had become so dependent on domesticated crops that desperate attempts to switch to wild plant and animal foods met with little success, especially since drought also affected the canyon's wildlife. Surviving Pueblo oral traditions from more recent times record previous drought cycles in vivid narrative. Had the drought lasted for a couple of years, the Chacoans would have recovered, but these dry cycles were longer.

As drought conditions worsened, food became scarcer, and more crops failed. There is evidence of a great deal of suffering as food supplies dwindled and water was increasingly contaminated, revealed by studies of skeletons from a small settlement where malnutrition and backbreaking work had taken a heavy toll. Many children had severe iron-deficiency anemia, which increased the risk of dysentery and respiratory disorders. Poorly nourished women were often unable to reproduce frequently enough to maintain their households. To people who lived stoically through the drought, it must have seemed that the forces of the supernatural had deserted them, that their leaders were ineffective mediators between the living, the gods, and the ancestors. At Chaco, rainfall was the driver of society, impervious to ritual, however elaborate.

Within a few generations, the Great Houses and small Chaco settlements were almost empty. The people had fallen back on an ancient strategy: that of movement, closely linked to social ties that extended far beyond Chaco Canyon. Such connections meant that, though the people clearly suffered, there was no immediate mass migration out of Chaco. Instead, the pueblos and villages were gradually abandoned. There was constant movement in and out of the canyon: people would leave for a season, decide to return, or dwell with kin in the highlands for a while. Some Chacoans lived like this until the fourteenth century, regularly returning to their base, where they would tend their gardens and maintain their rights over water supplies, while also forging wide links with communities for hundreds of miles around. It was these very ties that probably enabled their gradual migration out of the region, as people moved south, possibly to Mesa Verde, and toward the Hopi, Zuni, and Rio Grande pueblos.

The impact of climate change on life in Chaco Canyon has long been discussed. Had the Chacoans' intensive agriculture played a role? Had the construction of the Great Houses, which required large numbers of wooden beams, deforested the region and destabilized the landscape? How people responded to the droughts is strongly debated. Did they in fact pull together by drawing on long-held community and kinship ties, or were they violent, or both? Indeed, were there powerful elite groups living in the Great Houses and, if so, what sort of control did they exert over the people as conditions changed?

The now deserted, once vibrant, Chaco Canyon is often used as an ecological warning for the future. Though the past does not reliably predict the present, it can offer useful insights into the possible ways that people have responded to change. In this case, perhaps not dissimilar to modern examples of migration in the face of economic or ecological hardship, the story is one of resilience, and of strong community and kinship ties, which ultimately facilitated the gradual move out of a region that was no longer sustainable.

The story of Chaco Canyon shares a number of parallels with the ancient Maya of Central America. The Maya are known for their spectacular ceremonial centers, elegantly painted pottery, and elaborate script, deciphered in one of the great archaeological achievements of the twentieth century. Maya civilization was a patchwork of competitive city-states, constantly at war or in ever-changing alliances, ruled by dynasties that claimed genealogical links to revered ancestors. Great centers, such as Copán and Tikal, with their plazas and pyramids, were models of the Maya cosmos, their societies pyramid-like with rulers at the top, nobles, and then commoners, where the many worked for the few. The Maya were consummate farmers and water managers, who relied on irrigated swamp gardens, rainfall from unreliable precipitation, and ponds to support dense populations that produced maize and other crops from only moderately fertile soils. Their city-states prospered until the ninth century AD, when much of lowland Maya civilization appears to have collapsed. Many centers, including Copán and Tikal, were abandoned; the people scattered into the small villages where they maintained kin ties. In their rural communities, they were free of obligations to provide food and labor to the elite lords, who were now virtually powerless. This made survival at a basic level a viable adaptation. Only in the northern Yucatan did Maya civilization flourish until European contact in the fifteenth century.

Endless books and scientific papers have been written about what is often called the "Classic Maya collapse." Climatically, what is known from cores bored into the deposits of fresh water lakes that measure rainfall fluctuations is that a series of intense drought cycles descended on the Maya lowlands at fifty-year intervals during the ninth century. Maya civilization was increasingly vulnerable to drought after centuries of major population growth and intensified agricultural production that extended even onto less fertile soils. One cannot say that climate change *caused* the collapse, for it was clearly a highly complex process. What is fascinating is that increasing vulnerability to drought, with all the suffering that implies, was dealt with by people moving away from centralized cities and dispersing into their traditional villages, where local kin ties reigned.

Rulers, States, and Climate Change

So far, we have explored local responses, and ties between people, but what about much larger-scale societies? These tend to have ancient written and illustrated sources in addition to what we can glean from archaeology and climatology. As a result, we know that, for the Ancient Egyptians, the Sumerians, the Maya, and others, most food production lay in the village, even if the crops were grown for urban markets under close official supervision.

Vulnerability to climatic shifts was always local, even for a complex state like Old Kingdom Egypt, which depended on annual Nile river floods to fertilize and water the agricultural land that fed the state. In around 2100 BC, the region suffered a century or more of very poor flooding, which decimated agricultural production. The Egyptian state soon fell apart in the face of political chaos and hunger. Only the most powerful and competent provincial rulers (nomarchs) prospered, for they controlled local grain supplies. The nomarch Khety of Asyut in Upper Egypt boasted in his tomb inscriptions that he built temporary dams to retain floodwater and rationed grain. "I was rich in grain when the land was a sandbank and nourished my town by measuring grain." He and his contemporaries knew that only draconian measures would work, and distributed grain with care to prevent hunger. The state itself effectively no longer existed; survival depended on local responses by leaders who had themselves deep roots in the countryside. As for the pharaohs, they had proclaimed that their divine associations enabled them to control Nile floods. They were shown to be powerless in the face of much lower river levels that failed to water the land along its banks. It was no coincidence that later rulers called themselves "shepherds of the people" and invested heavily in irrigation and grain storage. These rulers survived for two thousand years.

In exploring past societies, archaeologists often discover how far the elite would go to make people follow them—regardless of whether these men and women did so willingly or unwillingly. It was, after all, in their economic and social interest to have the masses under their control: the many subservient to the few. The elite would write their authority into laws, which would be upheld by rituals, and sanctioned by the gods. In a dangerous world, as when beset with major environmental challenges, people would sometimes follow their leaders to the death.

The Moche, who lived on the northern coast of Peru from around the second to eighth centuries AD, provide a chilling case in point. The Moche subsisted off anchovies from the sea, along with maize, and beans grown in irrigated fields fed by mountain-water run-offs from the Andes. Yet the area was (and still is) affected by major El Niños, the warming of ocean water in the southwestern Pacific that causes short-term yet major climatic shifts—such as major floods or intense droughts—in widespread areas of the world. The warrior-priests of the Moche state in AD 400 were well aware of El Niños that could wipe out generations of irrigation works in a few hours. Such destruction, which would have coincided with a drastic reduction in anchovy populations as a consequence of inshore Pacific currents, threatened their grip on the farmers that supported them.

The painted walls of the priests' great temple at Huaca de la Luna in the Lambayeque Valley bear depictions of local species, such as octopuses and sea lions, affected by El Niño events, and depict reliefs of animals associated with El Niños. The elite Moche warrior-priests wore pectoral decorations, bracelets, and other ornaments featuring creatures that arrived off the coast only when the El Niño countercurrent was flowing (see Plate 3). These decorative objects were their badges of honor—in artwork people are shown adorned with these symbols and at death they were buried and covered with them. It seems that the rulers evoked the major El Niño events to reinforce their authority at times of crisis. They further magnified their potency by engaging in brutal ceremonies that involved human sacrifice, their victims left sprawled in the temple precincts. Sadly the weather failed to take note of the ritualized dramatics. Eventually, the people moved upstream, farther away from the ocean, but around AD 650, another massive El Niño, and severe drought cycles, undermined the Moche state beyond recovery.

The rulers of the later Chimor state, which established itself on the same northern coast of Peru in the ninth century AD, approached things very differently. This society had the pressures of droughts and El Niños etched into its very existence. The Chimu rulers combated this reality, and that of a rapidly growing population, by intensive investment in closely organized, highly diversified agriculture, using forced labor to create a huge network of canals that joined neighboring valleys—some of the artificial waterways were 25 miles (40 kilometers) long. Careful timetables governed the distribution of precious water supplies. These were long-term considerations, based on an utterly frank appraisal of a brutal, unpredictable, and very dry environment (except in El Niño years). One is struck by the success of such forward planning by the rulers of Chimor, who thought wisely about food and water shortages on a broad scale—and did something about the situation.

For many centuries, the Chinese rulers also invested in ambitious water schemes. Effective water management in imperial China depended on strong, proactive leadership, both in the emperor's administration and locally. An official of the Qing dynasty, Chen Hongmou (1696–1771), served in more than a dozen states across the emperor's domains. He was an expert bureaucrat who paid close attention to local terrain and crop patterns. Above all, he built irrigation systems to endure, despite the expense. In the mountainous Yunnan Province in southwestern China, he constructed a series of reservoirs regulated by several dams to collect rainwater. At the same time, he ordered the provincial magistrates to survey the terrain and water flows of their districts, and compiled a hydraulic atlas. He then divided the region into sectors, creating a complex network of corruption-free assessments, government loans, and rental-income payments to fund a network of tile gutters and bamboo pipes that irrigated wide tracts of fields using gravity and strategically placed waterwheels. All of this was constructed to last, and survived into recent times. The scale of his projects seems almost incredible, until one realizes that he had almost unlimited labor at his disposal.

Chen argued that extensive water-management projects were in the general interest, he was proactive with maintenance and repairs, and fostered a sense of teamwork, relying on archives to check how systems operated over many generations. He had been schooled in a tradition of extensive water projects involving thousands of people. The strategy of deploying large numbers of people on these highly ambitious projects worked for a while, until rising population densities and agricultural production during the eighteenth century fell out of balance. The labor required to reverse the damage wrought by floods and droughts over the years, alone, was unsustainable.

Lessons from the Past

Some important lessons for today and the future can be drawn from these and many other examples of human responses to climate change. Of course, we cannot use ancient climatic change to predict the future, but the important point is that we can use archaeology to study human reactions to short- and long-term climatic shifts at a time when our vulnerability to such changes as rising sea levels is higher than ever before. Today, tens of millions of people live close to, or even slightly below, sea level, at the mouths of great estuaries, or in cities with populations in the millions. They do so in an era when such extreme weather events as hurricanes with their lethal sea surges, heavy rainfall, and much greater aridity, are facts of life in a warming world.

Our predecessors some 6,000 years ago still had the option to move away in the face of environmental change. They maintained links with others near and far in landscapes where fewer people dwelt. Our vulnerability has increased exponentially with the growth of cities and their burgeoning populations, mostly comprising non-farming specialists and other workers who were controlled by increasingly elaborate bureaucracies. Finally, as a result of the Industrial Revolution, we are at the point of crisis. We cannot simply up and move like the people of Doggerland. We would struggle to evacuate entire cities with populations in the millions. Yet, compared with our ancestors, we live in a global world of interconnection and rapid communication. For the first time, we are all in the same climatic boat. Fortunately, we also have the value of modern science, which can tell us so much.

Looking back to the past, there is much we can learn from it. We can see the things we did wrong—such as not dealing with the real issues, and instead preferring to focus our attention elsewhere, as, for example, when the Moche dressed up in sea-creature costumes while sacrificing people. But we can also witness the things that worked—such as the cooperative and strategic approach to the land shown by the traditional Yemeni terrace farmers. At such times as these, archaeology fills us with hope and reminds us that perhaps the greatest trait of *Homo sapiens* is that we are an adaptable species, as any human evolutionist would agree.

Climatically, we are in a new era, where we, the self-same *Homo sapiens*, are now the agents of climate change on a massive scale. The threats that confront us are open-ended in an ever more densely populated world where tens of millions of people face chronic food shortages caused by aridity. In the past, climate change affected societies large and small, simple and complex, but they were usually able to adapt, thanks to ties of kin and an ability to maintain contacts with their rural roots. The only solutions lie in our ingenuity as human beings—long-term planning, and aggressive yet cooperative steps to prepare for further change. Above all, we need to develop societies that thrive on long-term planning, not election cycles, and that take steps now to make the world better for future generations. This will require levels of altruism, caring, leadership, and concern for people globally in other societies, who also have a stake in the future. The threat of climate change on an unprecedented scale makes one realize that, for all the frenzied protests of politicians, nationalism and xenophobia are dying preoccupations as humanity wakes up to ideas of global unity in the face of common, life-threatening, ecological challenges. Fortunately, an archaeological perspective on deep history shows us that when humans are really up against things, we do take action—and this should give us hope for the future.

Figure 4. The conical tower and monumental drystone walls of Great Zimbabwe, built in the thirteenth to fourteenth centuries AD. Colonial historians once argued that the settlement was built by non-Africans, but archaeological research and oral traditions have proven it to have been built by ancestors of modern-day Africans.

3 Revealing Who We Are

Who are we? Where do we come from? How did we live? Archaeology, with its massive time span, widens the lens far beyond the narrow confines of the history books, allowing us to build a uniquely rich picture of human experience. It has the ability to give a voice to all those without written history—from those who lived in deep prehistory to those of more recent times who did not write. By exploring people from every time, country, culture, class, age, or gender, archaeology has the power to demolish assumptions and prejudiced stereotypes about what it means to be human. This chapter is mostly about telling some of the untold stories of our forebears, but it will begin by returning to the fundamental question of our origins. This is, of course, a subject that draws heavily on the work of other scientific disciplines, notably genetics and biological anthropology.

The intellectual dangers that threaten any analysis of our ancestry are formidable: ethnocentrism, racism, and imperialism. Many of these issues originate in colonial-era convictions that human societies evolved from the simple to the complex in a linear, orderly fashion, with white Europeans at the top. This, seemingly, made it perfectly acceptable for the European colonists to dominate and/or enslave all those with darker skins who were generally regarded as far inferior.

But then came nineteenth-century research into human origins and biological diversity, which began with the work of Charles Darwin and Thomas Huxley, and the surprising discovery of the beetle-browed Neanderthal "ape men" in Europe. There were vigorous debates over whether we were in fact descended from the apes, something that seemed absolutely impossible when set against the divine words of scripture, which decreed that "God created man in His image" (Genesis 1.27).

The origin of *Homo sapiens* was, and perhaps still is, a controversial subject. Even just a few generations ago, researchers thought of human evolution in terms of yet another ladder of progression, with missing links, which began with an "ape-human," *Australopithecus*, in eastern and southern Africa, and proceeded in linear succession to *Homo erectus*, the Neanderthals, and finally us, *Homo sapiens*. In reality, things were rather more complex. We now know that over the past six or seven million years, more than twenty hominin species walked the earth, with various forms preceding the australopithecines, and several typically coexisting at any given time. The precise relationship between the various species is, however, often unclear, and evolutionists' resultant models certainly don't resemble neat ladders. Even the European Neanderthals, originally assumed to be our progenitors, are now known to be our cousins, with whom we shared a common ancestor in Africa.

Debates also raged concerning our homeland. Where did modern humans come from? Did we originate from one place, or did we arise in many? And to what extent were people living at opposite ends of the earth related? The disputes revolved around two major models: the multi-regional hypothesis, and the "Out of Africa" theory.

In 1947, a biological anthropologist, Franz Weidenreich, suggested that modern humans had originated in many areas of the Old World. Our ancestors were the upright, primordial human *Homo erectus* but, because of gene flow (the open mixing of people across regions), the evolving regional populations were essentially the same, resulting, in the end, in a single human species. Weidenreich's ideas became fashionable and developed into what became known as the multi-regional hypothesis. The model assumes that modern differences in our looks and our biology have very deep roots in the past. The idea lends itself to a racial interpretation more in line with nationalist ideology, and white supremacist circles—and some governments—have been known to draw on the work of authors with multi-regional approaches.

The second major *Homo sapiens* model was the Out of Africa scenario. In contrast to the multi-regional approach, it argued that *Homo sapiens* evolved in Africa and then spread to all the other parts of the Old World. It implied that modern geographic populations have shallow roots, and that we are all derived from a single source in relatively recent times. In the early 1990s, a burst of genetic and archaeological findings meant that most specialists were in favor of this approach.

Lately, these two camps have been joined by a third: intermediate scenarios that find support from even more recent genetic research. This third approach supports the Out of Africa perspective but has been refined to allow for some interbreeding, once we had left our African homeland, between *Homo sapiens* and other (now extinct) humans, notably with our Neanderthal cousins in Europe, and a set of poorly understood hominins known as the Denisovans in Asia. Despite the genetic variation in modern populations, all living humans are remarkably similar. And, although our looks may *seem* to vary, geneticists have shown that, whether we come from Wimbledon or Weifang, 99.9 percent of our genetic code is identical.

African Origins

All of the evidence points to an African origin for every modern human. But when did we leave Africa and how might we be related? Traditionally, archaeologists were reliant on fossils and artifacts to build timelines of human prehistory, but now they have access to genetic studies that are providing crucial information to the wider human story.

The major breakthrough has been the sequencing of the human genome. This means we can now make comparisons between humans from various parts of the world, which allows the study of evolutionary relationships between different populations and migration patterns. The idea of the "molecular clock" is central to this work. Molecular clocks are based on two main biological processes that are all heritable: mutation and recombination. Mutations are changes to the DNA's genetic code, which are then passed down to future generations—usually the result of mistakes when DNA copies itself during cell division. The changes number about seventy per generation and accrue like the ticks on a stopwatch. Since certain genetic changes occur at a seemingly steady rate per generation, they provide an estimate of time elapsed. When geneticists compare the DNA sequences of different groups, they can then reconstruct the relationships between the groups, and also infer evolutionary developments over deep timescales.

Recombination is the other main way that DNA accumulates changes over time. It leads to shuffling of the two copies of the genome (one from each parent) that are then bundled into one's chromosomes. The genome passed on to children is a mosaic of the parents' DNA, with about thirty-six recombination events per generation. Since this happens with every generation, segments inherited from a given person get smaller and smaller, allowing scientists to work out how long ago that individual was your ancestor. Genetic changes from mutation and recombination provide two distinct clocks but, given mutations accumulate more slowly, that clock is better for ancient events such as the splits between different species, while the recombination clock is better for events of the past 100,000 years. Though there are questions over the speed of the clocks, this work is helping to date our movement from Africa to Asia and Europe, and then into the Americas.

The implications of the various arguments, whether from genetics or archaeology, particularly when falsely used to argue for supposed racial supremacy, demonstrate how important this sort of research, and the archaeological questions surrounding our origins, can be. Indeed, on the subject of racial supremacy, archaeology has achieved a great deal in opposing such doctrines, particularly the assumption of ladder-like progress in ancient times. The vicissitudes of archaeological research at Great Zimbabwe are a classic example of the triumph of archaeology over racist ideology.

In 1868, a German-American prospector, Adam Render, stumbled on the brush-covered ruins of Great Zimbabwe north of the Limpopo river in southern Africa. Great Zimbabwe was the center of a powerful kingdom based on trade and cattle herding, which flourished from around AD 1000 to the early fifteenth century. In its heyday, about 800 years ago, thousands of people lived in villages clustered near the stone-walled Great Enclosure, with its distinctive conical tower (see Figure 4) and series of secluded stone enclosures on a hill known today as the Acropolis, which overlooked the crowded valley below. Chiefs known as the Mwene Mutapa ruled over Great Zimbabwe, which was a major trading center for gold, ivory, and other commodities exchanged for such exotic items as cotton cloth brought inland from the east coast by caravans.

Render was astounded by Zimbabwe's high stone walls, built of carefully shaped granite blocks. He showed them to Karl Mauch, a German geographer, four years later. Convinced that no African could have built Zimbabwe, Mauch proclaimed that he had found the ancient palace of the biblical

Queen of Sheba. A local journalist, Richard Hall, dug into Zimbabwe's Great Enclosure in 1901. He found gold beads, copper ingots, and imported porcelain, and announced that a great Mediterranean civilization had indeed once flourished deep in the African bush. His theories were overtly racist and appealed strongly to the local European settlers, who saw his excavations as a justification for seizing African land.

At the time, any effort to show otherwise was laughed to scorn. So passionate were settlers' feelings that it was not until 1929 that the British Association for the Advancement of Science sent a well-qualified excavator to Zimbabwe. Gertrude Caton-Thompson arrived at the ruins in an ox cart; she was a formidable personality and an expert at dissecting complicated sites. She dug deep into stone-bound sections of the Acropolis hill overlooking the site's Great Enclosure. Her trenches yielded fragments of Chinese porcelain dating to between the fourteenth and fifteenth centuries AD. This made the site far later than any supposed for the Old Testament Queen of Sheba, disproving this particularly colonial theory. Furthermore, she proposed that Great Zimbabwe was of Bantu origin, constructed by a native African society. A torrent of abuse descended on Caton-Thompson's head, but her critics had met their match. She dismissed their claims out of hand and stored their correspondence in a file labeled "insane."

Great Zimbabwe is now widely accepted as the work of Africans and is a prime example of how archaeology can dissolve theories and assumptions that are grounded in, and perpetuate, racist attitudes. Such theories about Great Zimbabwe persist on the fringes of debate to this day despite generations of careful archaeological research and argument. The battle for a more diverse picture of human history is far from over.

The ultimate lesson from the past is crystal clear. We *Homo sapiens* may be a diverse species, but that diversity does not reflect any innate mental superiority or inferiority between different groups and societies, merely different ways of facing the challenges of short- and long-term existence. Indeed, this adaptability is perhaps our greatest strength. We've always had many ways of doing things. If there is no need for us to adapt and change then we won't. But, particularly when we are up against some form of pressure, we usually do. Sometimes this change is incremental, and sometimes rapid. The collaboration of archaeologists, biological anthropologists, and geneticists is revolutionizing the study of human adaptation as we know it.

Our long history of adjusting to widely diverse local environments, and to climate change, were all-important factors in fostering our cultural diversity and similarity but, as happens today, not everyone in the past had equal access to food, resources, or freedom. The pasts of those exploited or subjugated groups are less known in written history, and so archaeology can offer a window that enhances and diversifies our image of the past.

People without History

A great deal of archaeology unearths forgotten people of the past, whose history was never written down. While some crucial oral records survive, much has been lost. Archaeologists help to piece together the history of such people, whether members of small ancient hunting groups, workers laboring to erect prehistoric monuments, or anonymous nineteenth-century miners or railroad workers living in camps in rugged western American terrain.

Chinese laborers constructed much of the transcontinental railroad of North America. Many of them occupied Summit Camp near Donner Summit in California from 1865 to 1869. The laborers worked under daunting conditions, leveling the land, excavating seven tunnels using explosives and picks, and laying hundreds of miles of railway track. Most labor camps used tents and temporary structures, but the Chinese workers at Summit Camp built a modest-sized town with permanent small cabins to protect them against the cold. While some of the workers were probably literate, no written documents by them have yet been found, and almost nothing remains of Summit Camp today. Archaeologists have been working to put together evidence of the workers' lives, and were able to match one cabin shown in a historical photograph with its surviving stone foundation and its hearths. Artifacts recovered around the cabin included coins, Chinese and American tableware, distinctive opium pipe fragments, and gaming pieces. The researchers also identified an almost cylindrical hearth, up against a hillside, which was probably used for cooking whole animals, such as pigs. Microfloral and other tests of nearby soil revealed that the inhabitants had consumed barley, rice, and legumes, as well as local elderberries and bearberries. Historical records from American officials tell us that the laborers ate dried oysters and abalone, and a variety of other foodstuffs. They also brought in catfish that thrived in a nearby lake. Written history tells us very little of the day-to-day of these people, but archaeology can offer us at least a small glimpse.

Archaeologist William Evans studied Chinese artifacts from Summit Camp, and from as far away as Ventura and Riverside in southern California, and Virginia City in Nevada. He found a remarkable standardization of table wares, what he called the paraphernalia of subsistence and relaxation—opium and gambling. The items associated with Chinese workers varied remarkably little from one location to another and were associated almost entirely with male laborers. Only in Virginia City, where women and children were present, did the items show more variation. The Summit laborers may have been anonymous, isolated players in local history, but their distinctive Chinese artifacts, such as eating vessels, reveal a culture of outsiders who maintained close contacts with other Chinese communities.

Such archaeological projects articulate the history of the voiceless. Further work exploring otherwise forgotten Chinese migrant laborers is currently being undertaken at Stanford University through the Chinese Railroad Workers in North America Project. This major venture seeks to uncover the stories of thousands of Chinese incomers who worked to complete the railroad between 1865 and 1869. Collaborating with the Chinese Historical Society of America and Chinese colleagues, the project draws on textual, oral, as well as archaeological sources, and works hard on outreach to increase awareness of this lesser-known part of American history.

The term "people without history" covers a multitude of different societies, some well known in the history books. Tens of thousands of people labored anonymously for emperors, pharaohs, and rulers of all kinds. Many lived out their lives in what was effectively indentured labor or slavery, so that we forget that many ancient cities were vibrant, highly diverse places, where thousands of humble and less oppressed folk with common occupations or close kin ties clustered in enclaves. Entire urban quarters in Mesopotamian cities, such as Ur in southern Iraq, housed largely self-sufficient communities of people from afar, many of them merchants or specialist artisans with strong connections in the countryside. Standardized pottery styles, architectural traditions, and other material remains mask the often wide diversity of ancient life in all its anonymity.

Ancient Egyptian laborers lived away from the spotlight of palace and temple. Illiterate, usually with short life expectancy, they passed through life without celebration or distinction (see Figure 5). Vital information about the real lives of Egyptian commoners comes from the short-lived city of Amarna, commissioned by the heretic pharaoh Akhenaten after he came to the throne around 1350 BC.

Akhenaten created Amarna as a new city devoted to the cult of one god, the solar deity, Aten. Though the pharaoh wasn't quite a monotheist, he was certainly moving in that direction, having audaciously rejected the Egyptian pantheon of gods in favor of Aten. Built on an otherwise barren bay of desert on the east bank of the River Nile, midway between Cairo and Luxor, Amarna was home to an estimated 30,000 to 50,000 people: officials, soldiers, servants, craftsmen, and builders, all of whom served the royal court. Soon after Pharaoh Akhenaten's death, around 1335 BC, however, Amarna was rapidly rejected as a city as the priesthood sought to reinstate the status quo in Egypt. Soon overlain with sand, the abandoned city (first identified by archaeologists in the nineteenth century AD) is providing us with a unique snapshot of life in the fourteenth century BC. And while ancient art shows Amarna as a place of plenty, ongoing excavations are revealing that the lives of the workers and commoners were far from paradise.

On the south side of the city, the current team has found the cemeteries of the ordinary people who formed about 90 percent of the population. So far, over 500 graves have been excavated, containing around 535 sets of human remains. Most burials were devoid of any grave goods, apart from perhaps a few beads, amulets, or other trinkets. Many of the skeletons show signs of dietary deficiency, disease, and heavy workloads—there are numerous examples of spinal trauma, including painful fractured and compressed vertebrae, proof of brutally hard work, much of it carrying stone blocks. These were not people who were growing old in comfort: the average age of death for those who survived into adulthood was in the early thirties, with damage to the bodies of children over the age of seven providing evidence that they, too, were routinely put to hard labor. Theirs was nothing short of a brutal existence.

These people are without recorded history, save, perhaps, as a statistic in a bureaucrat or scribe's document, just like the laborers on nobles' estates (see Plate 4). Archaeology can not only shine a light on these people without history, but also expose the social inequalities beneath the veneer of pyramids and victorious kings.

Figure 5. Unceasing labor. A facsimile painting of a weaver's workshop from the Beni Hasan tomb of Khnumhotep III, an ancient Egyptian high official, *c.* 1897–1878 BC.

Diverse Stories

Archaeologists tell stories about the past, but unlike the historian who is focused on documentary and oral records, archaeology digs far deeper. It can conjure up personal and otherwise forgotten narratives from scatters of tools, house foundations, food remains, and myriad other clues that help us to gain a more rounded picture of the past.

The stories that can be told from archaeological finds can be truly extraordinary. Take, for example, the tale of Ötzi the Iceman from the Italian Alps, the earliest European to survive as an identifiable individual, his body having been preserved by glacial ice that flowed over it. He was 5 feet 2 inches (1.6 meters) high, and he died in a small gully, his possessions laid beside him, sometime between 3350 and 3150 BC (see Plate 5). Ötzi's body has yielded astounding detail, thanks to hi-tech medical science. Putting together isotopic signatures from his teeth, also traces of mica in his intestine, experts have determined that he was born in one of several river valleys of the southern Tyrol, and moved to higher altitudes when an adult. He suffered from malnutrition in his ninth, fifteenth, and sixteenth years, detected from radiographs of his bones that revealed the telltale "Harris lines" that are signs of malnutrition at different ages. Ötzi also had parasites, and was weak and hungry when he died. He seems never to have strayed further than 37 miles (60 kilometers) from his birthplace. On the day of his death, he wore a loin cloth and suspenders, a pair of fur leggings, an outer coat of animal skin, and a cape of twisted grass, just like those commonly worn in the Alps a century ago. He carried an axe, a bow and arrows in a quiver, a backpack, and was in a fight before he died, shown by DNA to have been with at least four people. He appears to have died from an arrow wound in his left shoulder.

We know more of Ötzi's medical history than he did, but even with all this forensic data, there is so much more one would like to know about the Iceman. His discovery sent a frisson of excitement through Europe. What was his ancestry? His mitochondrial DNA, inherited through his mother, showed that his maternal line apparently died out in the Alps, as the genetic lineage does not exist in modern people today. His Y chromosome, transmitted from father to son, comes from a genetic line still present in modern populations, known by a rare chromosome mutation known as G-L91. Perhaps his father came from central or northern Europe and passed through the area, Ötzi being the result of marriage or a romantic fling. At least nineteen relatives may still live in the Italian Alps.

Certainly, ancient societies were far more diverse, with greater cultural mixing over time, than is often assumed. Imperial Rome's population was a mix of foreigners from all corners of the empire, many of them slaves. Londinium, the city of London, was of course founded by "foreigners" (the Romans), and was always home to various waves of incomers from central and northern Europe, Africa, and beyond.

Archaeology's tools can reveal much more about non-literate people than can be gleaned from written or oral history. With forensic care, archaeology can add new dimensions to existing accounts, if not contradict them. Such was the case when researchers examined one of the most famous rebellions in American colonial history: the seventeenth-century Pueblo Revolt in New Mexico.

From 1540, Native American Puebloans were subject to incursions of Spanish settlers, missionaries, and soldiers. While Spanish policies outlined the humane treatment of the indigenous people, even from the first permanent colonial settlement in 1598, the Pueblos were forced to provide tribute to the colonists through labor, corn, and textiles, and any uprisings resulted in sometimes strong violence. For example, a rebellion at Acoma Pueblo in 1598 that resulted in the death of twelve Spaniards led to the slaughter of more than 800 Acoma.

Similar brutality lay behind the Pueblo Revolt almost a century later, in 1680, the biggest rebellion of its kind, which included most of the Pueblo communities in New Mexico. At its climax, a group of Jemez warriors jumped over a precipitous cliff to avoid the attacking Spaniards. The revolt had begun with the predictions of a charismatic Puebloan prophet named Po'pay, who declared that the Pueblo people would experience a better world if they wiped all traces of the Spaniards and their Christian god from their settlements. In August 1680, under Po'pay's lead, Pueblo people throughout northern New Mexico rose in revolt in an alliance with Apache and Navajo groups. They slaughtered twenty-one Franciscan missionaries and more than 300 colonial settlers. The locals celebrated their victory by destroying Christian churches, annulling Christian marriages, and washing off the stains of Christian baptism. They remained free until 1692, when New Mexico was brutally reconquered by the Spanish.

History, as we all know, is written by the conquerors, and is almost always biased in their favor. But how much of the defenders' story is accurate? Did the aforementioned Jemez warriors really leap off the cliff to their deaths? According to indigenous accounts, a likeness of the Saint Diego appeared on the cliff and caused some of the people to land on their feet and survive. Others recount that the saint eased their passage through the air so they "landed on the rocks like birds."

Archaeological and ethnohistorical research paint a different picture. We now know that eighty-four residents of the pueblo perished in the climactic battle. There seems no question, from oral accounts, that some of the jumpers did survive, and hid among the rocks. Excavations in the pueblo rooms recovered pieces of chain mail and copper plating from Spanish armor, dropped as they were smoked out of the chambers. But the mass suicide by jumping is partly a myth perpetuated by Pueblo storytellers, who wanted to give the people some sort of collective identity. After the revolt, there was an unspoken rapprochement between the Pueblos and the Spaniards, and a greater tolerance of traditional religious practices. Brutal exploitation on plantations ceased and the ancient religion survived into the modern world.

Overt defiance against oppressors is rare compared with more passive resistance, and archaeology uncovers the countless ways subversion and resistance can take place. North American slave plantations were complex networks that linked planter to planter, planters to slaves, and slaves to one another. Despite harsh, racist environments, many slave communities maintained their own beliefs and culture, holding that this was the best way to live. Such resistance flourished through secret religious activities. People covertly prayed to their own gods and incised African-origin religious symbols onto their possessions. There are well-documented examples of spirit bundles placed in pits or enclosed spaces that sought to protect the living from powerful forces that might harm the bundles' owners. These were forms of symbolic violence that were an effort by slaves to control the activities of their masters, perhaps even do them real harm. Written history does not tell their story on their own terms, but their artifacts do.

A cramped dwelling attached to the Lott house in the center of New York housed twelve slaves until 1810. The discovery of a space below the floorboards yielded twelve corn cobs set in a cross or star pattern, a carefully preserved, empty cloth pouch, and other items associated with Hoodoo, a North American variant of Vudon, a West African cult. In Annapolis, excavators found a dozen caches of items created by slaves living in houses owned by wealthy people between 1720 and 1920. They contained cult objects, sacred bundles with revered artifacts, such as beads and ornaments that preserved traditional African beliefs.

One of the most famous examples of the reclaiming of African-American history and the slave experience is the African Burial Ground in New York, discovered in 1991 during construction work. In Lower Manhattan, 419 individuals were uncovered and identified as African-American people who had been buried together in the eighteenth century. Initially, the construction plans were simply to exhume and preserve the remains while proceeding with the project, but protests and political interventions led to the suspension of building and the revision of plans. Now a $4.4 million visitor center occupies the site. Within its galleries, archaeologists and historians have aimed to put the burials in their proper context, to tell the story of the first large-scale evidence of black American experience in this part of the United States, and—as per the opening lines of its permanent exhibition—to "Reclaim Our History."

Finding the Hidden

Archaeology can tell us more about who we are precisely because it can give life to the silenced groups: the people omitted from the history books, or ignored by the elite narratives. At times, however, it can be hard to find them, sometimes because the very categories we are searching for are constructs of our present time. For example, a long, dependent, school-going childhood, replete with distinctive merchandise, gadgets, and clothes, is a modern Western construct. In Ancient Egypt, non-elite children were expected to be contributing members of society from around the age of seven. This means that sometimes it can be hard to find material culture that was clearly intended for, or associated with, everyday Egyptian children. Often it is only their bones that can tell us about their lives.

A recent study of almost 5,000 English children's skeletons dating from AD 1000 to 1700 has revealed much about the reality of life during King Henry VIII's social and religious Reformation. This work indicated that it was the king's new order that caused the single greatest negative change in childhood health, worse even than the effects of the Black Death, War of the Roses, or the Hundred Years' War. During the critical years of change, between 1530 and 1550, the team noted how signs of skeletal stress and disease in children almost doubled, while signs of trauma trebled. The problems were likely linked to the cessation of the social welfare provided by the Catholic Church: those children who would previously have been given alms, education, shelter, and medical care, suddenly found themselves receiving no formal support—a situation worsened by harvest failures, famine, and a heightened cost of living that produced widespread social disorder. The young bones offer rare insights into the lives of some of the most vulnerable members of society during this time of cultural and religious upheaval. These children of poverty would otherwise have no history, and their stories would not be told. The Church of England ultimately marched triumphant against the old Catholic ways, yet the reality it brought with it was far from glorious for these children.

Archaeology excels in the everyday realms of villages and small towns, tiny fishing settlements and hunting camps. It considers the full sweep of human existence—a great deal of which was previously hidden and unknown. It looks at our origins, and brings to light the forgotten, the marginalized, the poor, the ancient, and all other unrecorded people of the past. Much of the deep history of humankind has unfolded among such anonymous folk. This is why looking back at the past without archaeology in the equation is unthinkable.

Figure 6. The male-dominated past. An artist's impression of a Neanderthal group. This is very much a male interpretation, with assumed gender division, the male as hunter, and the female as caregiver.

4 Exploring Gender

We opened the previous chapter with some of the big questions of archaeology: Who are we? Where do we come from? How did we live? To which we might now add: How did we behave and why? Yet discovering how and why we acted in certain ways is one of archaeology's toughest challenges. After all, getting inside the heads of other people today, let alone those of our long-departed ancestors, isn't always easy. Moreover, to assess past behavior, we have to be critically aware of our modern biases and assumptions in order to avoid imposing our own cultural norms onto the past. The trouble is, some ideas are so firmly hardwired into us that we assume them to be innate, rather than societal convention. How we think about gender, the subject of this chapter, is a case in point.

Gender issues are, of course, currently very much in the limelight. But with ongoing political and legal clashes over what is natural or moral, as deep-rooted sexual inequalities are exposed, and as many people fight to define their own gender identities, what can archaeology add to the debate? In fact, our work is challenging some of our most deep-seated beliefs about sex and gender. Before we explain how, a few words on what we mean when we talk of sex and gender, terms that are often used interchangeably in everyday modern speech (itself an insight into how we view things).

Sex refers to our biology. It describes the anatomy of an individual's reproductive system and secondary sex characteristics developed during puberty. At its most common, our sex is either male or female. Yet biologists estimate that somewhere between 1 in 1,500 and 1 in 2,000 births are of children whose genitalia don't fit conventional male–female assignations. Depending on the criteria employed, the number of intersex infants may even be as high as 1 in 100 (Joyce, 2008). Likewise, chromosomal sex and sex hormones also range more broadly than the basic two-sex model of XX (normative female) and XY (normative male), with around 1 in 1000 to 1 in 2000 possessing alternatives such as XXY. On the other hand, gender is the cultural expression of what you and your society think it means to be a man, woman, intersex, non-binary, trans, or gender non-conforming. Your hair, clothes, pay, and even the level of intelligence you choose to display (or not) are all heavily gendered in our society, and pivot around the main man/woman division, so much so that we might forget that there are other ways of doing things.

Specifically within archaeology, studying sex is when we try to identify men and women from their skeletons. Studying gender is when we look at changing male, female, and intersex roles in the past. In this pursuit, our cultural baggage is heavy, and we need to be conscious of it. Let's begin by focusing on the language we use about the past.

The Male Narrative

Generations of fiction writers and scientists have written about "mankind" or the more generic term "man," much used in the 1930s and 1940s. Until relatively recently, archaeologists would routinely write of "Neolithic Man" or "Paleolithic Man," adding unselfconscious remarks such as "now man tamed fire" or "now man developed bows and arrows." This androcentric, or male-centered, terminology was so culturally ingrained that it seemed harmless, and perfectly natural. Yet the broad-brush use of the word "man" effectively wrote woman out of the picture. We never pictured any women chipping stones, or hunting ibex, or making discoveries. Women, if they were mentioned at all, were in the background, near invisible in the camp, perhaps doing a bit of plant gathering, child rearing, or serving their men in some way.

Notable, too, were the cultural assumptions of what it meant to be a man or a woman. Thus, any activity judged by archaeologists to be of high status—rock art, hunting, or tool making—would invariably be seen as the work of men. We'll explore this subject as this chapter unfolds but, as a case in point, take a look at the image in on page 54. We can see how the brave man holds his hunting spear, ready to protect the group. In the background, dull-looking women cower in the safety of the cave with a child.

And so the dichotomy went: active, strong, public men; passive, weak, private women. This was what we believed it meant to be male or female in the past, since these were the preferred qualities bestowed on men and women by our own male-dominated world. Other ways of being a man or a woman, let alone any possibility that there might have been other genders or social divisions that were more important than one's biological sex, were either not considered or ignored.

A turning point came with the publication of a famous "Man the Hunter" conference at the University of Chicago in 1966, which concentrated on contemporary hunters and gatherers. Many of the talks stressed both multidisciplinary research and the need to study gender roles in order to begin to understand some of the different ways humans might behave within such societies. This remarkable meeting, and its resulting publication, highlighted first-hand observations of living groups, so demolishing several myths, among them the notion that hunter-gatherers were perennially on the verge of starvation. Numerous participants also questioned the long-held assumption that men were even the hunters, while women collected plant foods and remained close to home. For example, anthropologists working with indigenous groups in the Western Desert of Australia noted how the sexual division of labor was flexible, variable, and seasonally overlapping. At times, men focused on hunting kangaroo and emu, although failure was so high that these animals only accounted for about 10 percent of calories consumed. Women also occasionally hunted kangaroo but more often smaller animals. Men hunted larger prey to gain social and religious status, rather than to provide for a community. Hunting for subsistence was a role shared by both men and women. Such ethnographic examples illustrate how there is not always a sharp division between hunter and gatherer, or male and female, but a far more complex division of labor.

Today, many more archaeologists are looking at gender identity in its various forms; what it means to be human, a woman, or a man; how these identities were defined and realized in the past; and whether such categories were even present in previous societies. The current successes of gender research in archaeology began as part of the feminist movement of the 1960s and 1970s. Early research, notably that by Margaret Conkey and Janet Spector in the 1980s, argued that archaeologists were overlaying their own modern-day, Western gender norms onto past societies, for example in the assumed sexual division of labor. These pioneers did not have an easy time. In general, the (male-dominated) archaeological establishment did not take their work seriously. As one influential male archaeologist reflected in 1992, "[Gender archaeology is] a new racket for the girls" who are on a "bandwagon [that] shouldn't be allowed to roll too far." Yet the "bandwagon" has carried on rolling.

Some of the first practical work focused on historical archaeology, where researchers realized they knew a great deal about men's activities but nothing about women's. For instance, excavations in downtown Washington DC's Federal Triangle by archaeologist Donna Seifert in 1991 yielded evidence about nineteenth-century women who labored at home doing piecework or laundry that brought income into the household, while looking after their families. Seifert also gave an identity to the women who served the neighborhood's numerous brothels, showing how they lived and boarded in their workplace, and how they used their earnings to buy fine clothing, cosmetics, and pharmaceuticals. There were few kitchen artifacts and higher percentages of clothing adornments such as buttons, tobacco pipes (used by men), and also fewer sewing implements than in working households. The Seifert research shows how artifacts can be used to reveal and study a diversity of women engaged in different occupations. Their possessions and purchases reflected their day-to-day occupations in vivid ways that were undetectable in historical records. For the first time, archaeologists had given a presence to these previously overlooked women.

Adding women to the historical narrative was a major step forward, a foundation stone of an entirely new set of questions about the past. Yet what about the women doing the archaeology? Women's rights have long been on archaeology's gender program. Groups such as the online community "Trowelblazers" are among those seeking to increase the visibility of women in archaeology—both now and in the past. Nonetheless, it remains a hard fact that men dominate the leading positions both within academia and commercial archaeology, even if the gender ratios are now changing. In the US, for instance, the proportions of senior level males and females are slowly moving towards equality. Despite these modern disparities, which reflect wider patterns in society, the archaeology of gender is finally coming of age. Today more and more researchers understand the various roles played by women in the past, while also questioning their assumptions surrounding gender. With this in mind, let's visit Dolní Věstonice.

The Venus Figurines

Dolní Věstonice was occupied around 30,000 to 24,000 years ago, during the last Ice Age, in what is today the Czech Republic. It is a highly unusual site, for it contains not only the world's oldest-known architecture, but also the world's oldest-known ceramics. Its inhabitants were hunters who used the bones of mammoths and other herd animals to build a fence-like boundary, while they lived in huts also made from mammoth bone as well as stone, which they may have covered with animal skins. They produced thousands of clay artifacts, many depicting the local animals, such as lions, rhinos, owls, and mammoths, while some were of people, in a style that appears in a number of other late Ice Age European sites.

The clay figurines are almost certainly representations of women, given their undulating hips, breasts, and bellies (see Figure 7). But who were they? Since their first discovery in the early twentieth century, it was assumed that they were "Venus figurines," valued—or even worshiped—for their fertility. Some have even imagined them to be erotic aids, made for men by men, a sort of prehistoric version of *Playboy*.

Valuing women primarily for their reproductive capacities, however, reflects the status of women in patriarchal societies. In traditional patriarchies, whether Classical Greece or those living in the North-West Frontier of Pakistan today, a woman's primary value lies in her reproductive powers. The more children the better, particularly boys. For when land and goods are passed through the male line, the men need to ensure their lineage, hence the extreme focus on a female's fecundity. Yet all modern civilizations are patriarchic in set up, including our own. While modern Western women have more autonomy, they remain objectified, with great value laid on their looks, youthful sexuality, and bodies. Little wonder, then, that the overtly curvy Venus figurines have, quite naturally, been interpreted as sex goddesses.

If we wind back the clock and consider things from the perspective of someone living in the late Ice Age, with all the demands of a harsh environment, we can see how heightened fertility, with the result of too many children, may have been more of a negative than a positive, and not necessarily something to revere. If the idea of fertility existed at all, then, it would probably have included notions of protecting pregnant women, avoiding stillbirth, overcoming child mortality, and rearing children to adolescence. But as Reay Tannahill, historian and author of a classic book on

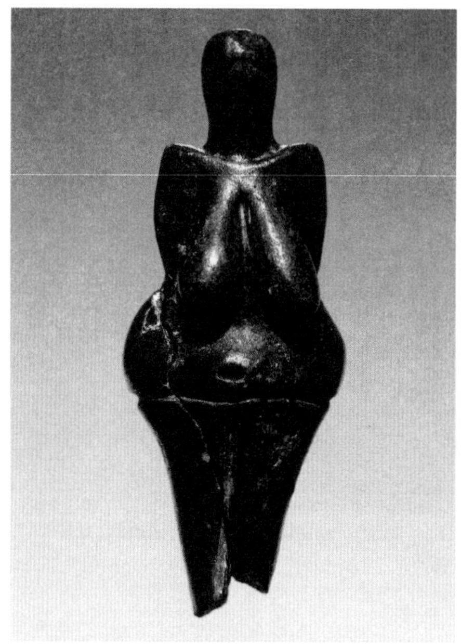

Figure 7. One of the nude female Venus figurines found at the Paleolithic site of Dolní Věstonice, Czech Republic. Among the world's oldest known ceramic objects, this statuette was made around 29,000 years ago.

sex, has observed, "It would have been an ambitious sculptor who attempted to crystallize all that into a four-inch statuette." Instead, argues Tannahill, if there were any interest in fertility, it would more likely have been focused on food supplies—whether fruit, tubers, seeds, nuts, legumes, or animals—rather than on women's reproductive powers.

Certainly, if we focus purely on the fertility element of the Venus figurines, we ignore other aspects of the statuettes. A closer look at them reveals more. Remember, they are the world's oldest known clay objects. To fire them required a kiln to produce temperatures as high as 1500 degrees Fahrenheit (815 degrees Celsius). But the clay was not left to dry fully, so steam caused a large number to explode. These explosions were so common that researchers think it was not a flaw, but a deliberate effect—that their firing was almost a performance. The purpose of the figurines may not have been to be kept, displayed, or revered, but to be deliberately destroyed.

Many Dolní Věstonice figurines also have textile impressions on them. Though the textiles have long since perished, the impressions show the people were also highly skilled in this regard. Were the figurines with these impressions self-portraits of the textile makers, made to celebrate their skills? After all, warm, well-made clothes may have been of more use to the group than a woman's fecundity. One figurine also bears a fingerprint, made by a child aged somewhere between seven and fifteen, which seems to have been a deliberate mark. Its meaning is unknown, but this is another clue that makes us wonder whether we have been focusing on the wrong things when we see these figurines purely in terms of female sexuality, fertility, or male eroticism, made by men and for men. Instead, careful analysis shows how our assumed ideas about gender and gender divisions have not always necessarily been set in stone—or clay.

Revising Assumptions

Debates over the Venus figurines continue, but in reconsidering these artifacts, archaeologists are highlighting our own biases surrounding gender. And such assumptions were once far from rare. In 1823, William Buckland, professor of geology at Oxford University and a creationist who believed that God created humanity six thousand years ago, was excavating in Goat's Hole Cave, a limestone cave in the Gower Peninsula, Wales. One week into his mission he found a skeleton daubed in red ocher and surrounded by bone jewelry and shell necklaces. Because of the elaborate ornamentation, he assumed the remains must be those of a woman, and he called her the "Red Lady of Paviland." Observing her red painted skeleton—the color associated with European brothels—he further concluded that she must have been a Roman prostitute, or maybe even a witch. As a man of his time, a witch or prostitute were clearly the only roles for an unusual scarlet woman. In fact, subsequent analysis has shown that the bones are actually those of a young male who lived around 33,000 years ago.

Another powerful example of how modern gender assumptions routinely imbued archaeological thinking is that of a Viking warrior found in Birka, Sweden, in the 1880s. The warrior was discovered lying buried with a cache of military items, among them a long bladed sword, a spear, and two sacrificed horses. On his lap were gaming pieces, suggesting he died while planning tactics (see Plate 6). This was clearly a man to be reckoned with. Or he was, until a 2017 DNA analysis of the warrior's bones confirmed beyond doubt that the grave actually belonged to a woman. Interestingly, Viking lore had always hinted that not all warriors were men, with one early tenth-century Irish text speaking of the "Red Girl," a female warrior who led a Viking fleet to Ireland. Likewise, many sagas tell of shield-maidens, who fought alongside male warriors—although such stories were generally dismissed as mythological fiction. The reanalysis is pause for thought: this is one example of a female warrior long assumed to be male, so are there others?

There are certainly many other cases where androcentric research and assumptions have begun to lose credibility. In Australia, archaeologists of previous generations created a narrative of the past that virtually excluded women and children. For example, many scholars assumed that in the Paleolithic it was only men who made and used stone tools, not women, unless in exceptional circumstances. In fact, numerous ethnohistoric accounts indicate that women as toolmakers and tool users were ubiquitous in all environments and in all regions of Australia. This was not a phenomenon exclusive to Australia, with women playing similar roles in other hunter-gatherer groups, such as among the Gamo and Konso people of southern Ethiopia.

Australian Aboriginal rock art is justly famous and that, too, was long supposed to have been produced by men. Yet again, ethnographic examples from northern Australia provided numerous instances of women creating rock art. Similar assumptions have been made about late Ice Age European rock art. As recently as 2005, a formidable tome on the art was published by a major university press, and written by an emeritus professor of zoology. The author's main argument is that the wondrous European Ice Age art was quite clearly the work of men, specifically testosterone-charged young men, owing to its focus on big game and bloody hunting scenes, its daring locations (often in the inner regions of caves), and because of the presence of Venus figurines, which he sees in terms of erotic aids. A recent reanalysis of the Ice Age hand images found in many of Europe's painted caves, however, is putting women in the picture. For when a team examined the morphology of stenciled hands from eight decorated caves in France and Spain, they observed that roughly 75 percent of them conceivably belonged to women (see Plate 7). The argument is based on the fact that women tend to have longer index fingers relative to their ring fingers, which links with the amount of testosterone received while in the womb. The results are far from secure but, at the minimum, this investigation raises the possibility that women could have been very much more involved in cave art activities than previously assumed.

A major lesson to be learned from such research is how easily gender assumptions can creep into interpretations of the past. As archaeologists increasingly reinterpret women's roles in previous eras, the ammunition for sex-based assumptions and categorizations turns to dust. Women have always existed, playing flexible and disparate roles, but it is only now that we are beginning to discern them fully.

Beyond Male and Female

While archaeologists have been writing women into the picture, some have gone further, questioning whether our preoccupation with the male–female divide was always valid. Might other factors, beyond one's sex, have been more important to the way people organized themselves? To explore this question, let's travel to the site of Tlatilco, on the edge of Mexico City.

Tlatilco had once been an agricultural village on the shore of Lake Texcoco that flourished from around 1200 to 200 BC. The original 1940s excavation team identified over 200 burials, many of which had intact grave goods. On cataloging these burials, the team blithely assumed that any differences in the grave goods corresponded with the sex of the dead person. Yet when archaeologist Rosemary Joyce revisited the site report catalog, she became worried. "Nothing I tested ended up being securely correlated with variation between men and women," she wrote in 2008. The only clear sex-related associations she could find were that some men were buried with unusual belts and ear spools, and more women wore necklaces. Yet even these assignations might not have been correct, since attribution of sex was based more on relative sizes of the bodies, rather than on definite skeletal information. Instead, Joyce found that the main differences between the graves were based on the ages of the deceased and not on sex. The highest number of objects, and the most unusual things, were routinely found in the burials of young adults. Perhaps the untimely deaths of these otherwise productive youngsters led to a coming together of the community, with more items being left in their graves. On the other hand, older men and women tended to be buried with clay rattle balls and with more varied body ornaments. In this village, if we assume that the graves provide a snapshot of the whole society, it seems that the male–female divide did not dominate their world, but rather people organized themselves according to age.

Who we are, and how we express ourselves, however, often changes within a person's own life cycle. As a consequence, the outward expression of what it means to be male or female can vary greatly even within a given society: the way a child expresses his or her gender—say through clothing or hairstyle—can be quite different to how the same person conveys femininity or masculinity as a twenty-year-old or an eighty-year-old. At other times, overarching social signifiers of gender can be fickle, sometimes changing in short order, with the potential to confuse even the most dedicated archaeologist. As a case in point, consider our own basic "time-honored" method for identifying and signifying boys and girls: blue is for boys and pink for girls. Yet it is worth remembering that this rule has very shallow roots, having only been codified in the West by children's merchandise manufacturers after World War II. A June 1918 trade journal observed how, "The generally accepted rule is pink for the boys, and blue for the girls. The reason [being] that pink, being a more decided and stronger color, is more suitable for the boy..."

Indeed, it is often far easier to examine flexible gender identities in the past *if* we have access to people's thoughts in the form of written information, whether historical accounts, or ethnographic records. There are plenty of ethnographic examples of native North American societies that describe shifting gender identity roles within a person's life. A new social identity would often be marked by initiation rituals such as the passing from adolescence into adulthood, where men and women would learn their culturally expected gender roles, imbued as they were with specific behaviors and duties. These accounts also tell of other gender identities that existed over and above the binary genders of men and women.

The Chumash Indians of southern California, like many Native American peoples, believed one's gender should be based on temperament, attitude, and preference for certain types of work. Western accounts from the time of European contact report that the Chumash were split into guilds, and that the guild of undertakers (*'aqi*) was open to people who identified themselves as neither men nor women—in other words, third gender individuals. Most *'aqi* were said to be men who wore women's clothing, but several reports indicate post-menopausal women were also involved. All of them were given a special spiritual status and, if they were sexually active, they engaged in non-procreative sex.

Plate 1. A replica of the Uluburun ship on the seabed off southern Turkey (see p. 21).
It was wrecked at the end of the fourteenth century BC.

(Above) Plate 2. The terraced fields of the Yemeni highlands. Terracing is an effective way of cultivating entire mountainsides, but its success depends on the careful cooperation of the whole community (see p. 29).

(Right) Plate 3. A stirrup vase designed as a portrait of a prominent Moche individual, perhaps a warrior priest. Moche potters were exceptionally gifted and modeled many details of local life, as well as ceremonial artifacts and portrait vases (see p. 36).

(Above) Plate 4. Social inequality: hard-working laborers bring in the grape harvest and process the crop on the estate of Nakht, a scribe and "Astronomer of Amun," *c.* 1380 BC (see p. 48). The painted tombs of important Egyptians often depicted idyllic scenes that were a far cry from reality.

(Right) Plate 5. Reconstruction of Ötzi the Iceman, based on minute examination of his frozen body (see pp. 49–50). Despite our knowing more about the Iceman's health than he did, there is still uncertainty as to his last few hours.

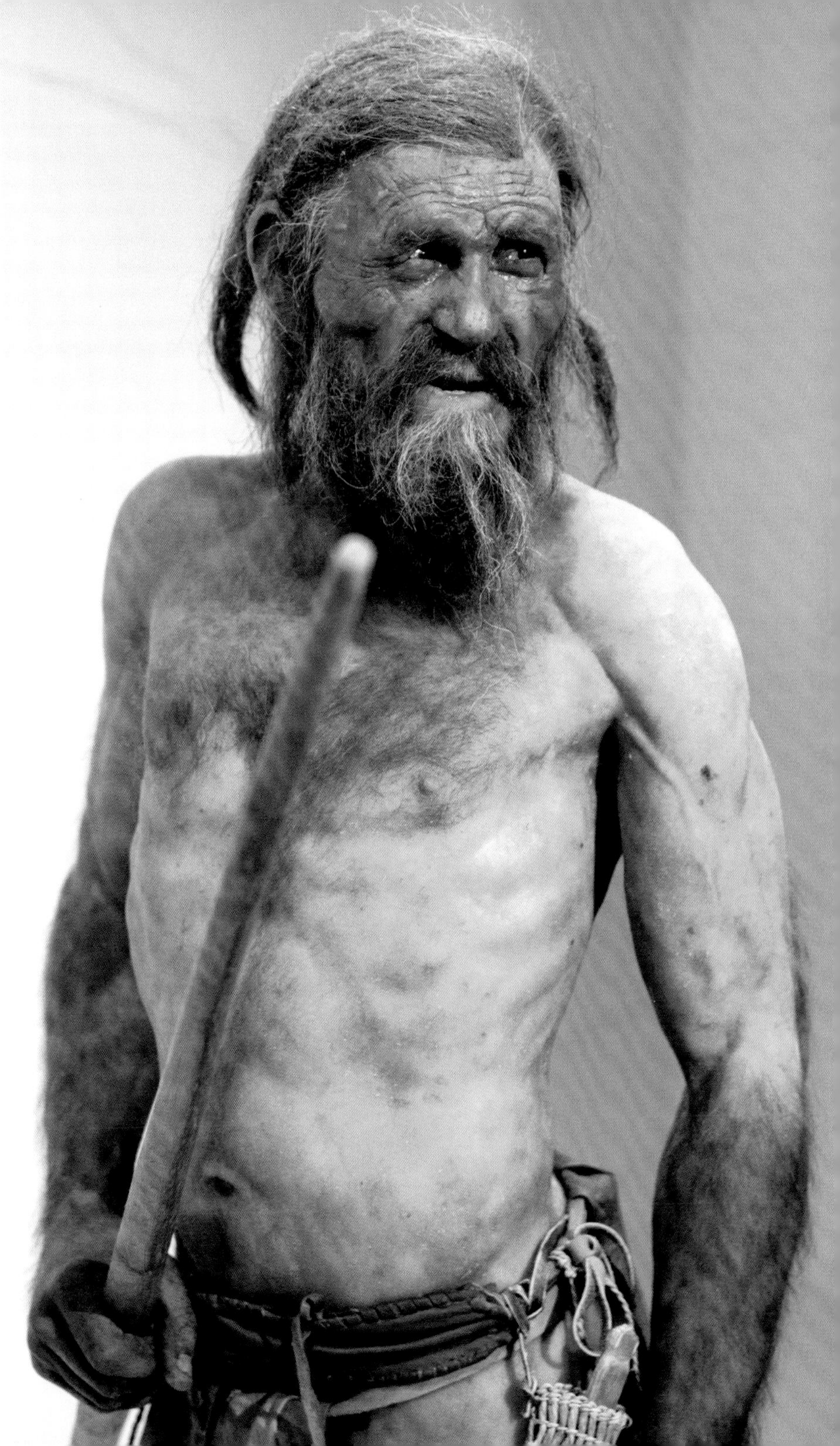

A
B
C
D
E
F
3 Fot.
1 Meter.
EVALD HANSEN.

(Left) Plate 6. The female Viking warrior found in Birka, Sweden: this is a sketch of her burial made by the original excavator, Hjalmar Stolpe, published in 1889. The warrior lies with a short battle axe, as well as gaming pieces, and has food offerings at her feet. Generations of researchers assumed she was male, but DNA has shown her to be a woman (see pp. 61–62).

(Above) Plate 7. Hand imprints and spotted horses from Pech Merle, Cabrerets, France. The date is unknown, but it is probably from around 17,000 years ago. Experts theorize that the owners of the hand imprints, which were made by blowing charcoal against the rock face, believed that these would enable them to gain supernatural powers from the animals lurking behind the wall.

Plate 8. The ritual bath on the citadel at Mohenjo-daro, Pakistan, one of the major cities of the Indus civilization. Steps led from a colonnaded courtyard into the brick-built, waterproof pool, which is 39 feet (12 meters) long, 23 feet (7 meters) wide, and 8 feet (2.4 meters) deep. It may have been used for religious purification.

Plate 9. A reconstruction of Cheddar Man, with his dark skin and blue eyes. DNA and sophisticated facial reconstruction methods from modern surgery have revolutionized our ability to re-create ancient people's appearances (see pp. 73–74).

(Left) Plate 10. A *moai*, an ancestral statue with red lava headdress and shell eyes, on Rapa Nui. Dozens of them were sculpted and set up, but exactly when is unknown, with AD 1600 a rough approximation. They were erected to look out over ancestral lands (see p. 81).

(Above) Plate 11. The Pyramids of Giza, built around 2550 BC, are probably the most-visited archaeological site in the world. The suburbs of Cairo now lap close to the pyramids, which were part of an elaborate mortuary complex.

Plate 12. Avebury stone circle, Wiltshire, England, from the air. The stone circle is part of a much larger sacred landscape, which includes burial mounds, enclosures, and a causeway. The modern village of Avebury (see p. 83) lies amid the site.

Plate 13. Tree roots engulfing a gallery at Ta Prohm temple, Cambodia, dedicated to the family of the ruler of Angkor (see p. 84). The inhabitants of numerous villages supported the shrine and consumed 38,000 tons of rice annually while performing the "service of the gods."

(Above) Plate 14. Bison at Niaux Cave, France, *c.* 12,000 years ago or earlier. The startlingly realistic paintings could well have been executed by artists sketching from a cliff above the dead animals, but this is speculation (see pp. 84–85).

(Right) Plate 15. A replica of a Moche Lord of Sipán, about thirty-five to forty-five years old, wearing his ceremonial regalia, and based on his burial in the Lambayeque Valley, Peru, *c.* AD 250. His golden headdress would have reflected the sun's rays at major public ceremonies (see p. 101).

Plate 16. The Parthenon, Athens, an iconic Classical temple, dedicated to the goddess Athena. The facade was once adorned with the iconic frieze removed by Lord Elgin and currently in the British Museum (see pp. 93–94).

Chumash ideology was rich in gendered concepts of many kinds, replete with both human and supernatural actors. But the *'aqi* had identities that mingled spirituality, their occupational expertise, and sexuality—aspects of personhood that were more important than either sex or gender. Archaeologist Sandra Holliman found two male Chumash skeletons of individuals who had died young, but whose spinal arthritis was different from that of other men. Their stressed spines looked identical to those of women who habitually used digging sticks and damaged their backs. Both men were buried with items found in men's graves, but also with baskets of the type usually interred with women. As a consequence, Holliman concluded that she had found physical evidence for the third-gender individuals, so supporting the evidence provided in the old historical accounts.

The Chumash were not alone in their inclusion of a third gender. Shamanistic practitioners in the past are often described as the equivalent of another gender. Among the nineteenth-century Chukchi in Siberia, the *yirka-lául* was a category of biologically male shamans who adopted first a female hairstyle, then female dress, and finally married males. They were feared by the rest of the Chukchi, as they were considered to be much more powerful than other shamans. An elaborate burial from the Ekven cemetery on the Bering Strait in the far north has been interpreted as a shaman burial. Dating to between 2000 and 2500 years ago, the owner of the grave was presented as a woman. However, she lay with bone, ivory, shell, and wood objects fashioned into both men's and women's tools—including drum handles and masks often associated with ritual practice. It was this mix of male, female, and ceremonial tools that has led archaeologists to identify the individual as a shaman, whose curing, ritual, and social roles were the equivalent to a third gender.

Recent research into ancient Pueblo people has explored other third-gender roles. The Zuni people use the word *Lhamana* to describe two-spirit or biologically male individuals who live in part as women and take up traditionally female tasks such as potting and weaving. Archaeologists are now examining pottery making in ancient pueblos and asking whether this practice is related to changing gender identity.

Digging Deeper

Most research on gender depends heavily on extrapolations from archaeological, ethnographic, or historical sources, and also from graves.

But there are other approaches that yield surprising dividends—among them, research into the food we ate.

The Sausa are long-term maize and potato farmers who live in Peru's northern Mantara Valley. In about AD 1460, their Sausa forebears came under the control of the Inca state. Their new masters, obsessed with control and agricultural production, dispersed the Sausa into smaller villages to encourage more efficient agriculture. Christine Hastorf is an expert on native South American plants and decided that this was a unique opportunity to study changing gender relations in a society transformed by conquerors.

Hastorf combined finds of plant remains in excavated dwellings with research in modern Sausa compounds. The pre-Inca structures yielded large quantities of a wide range of plant foods, including potatoes and legumes. Maize was found mainly in patio areas, where it was used both for food and to brew beer communally. Beer was a vital part of ritual, social, and political affairs. She then examined a later Inca-period compound, where there were fewer potatoes and much more maize. The corn processing was more concentrated, as if more of the maize was consumed as beer rather than food. The Sausa were by then living under Inca policies that sought a constant rise in maize production, and regular taxation in labor and produce. There was also a more intensified role for women in support of male activities.

Hastorf examined the male and female skeletons found in the compounds. Pre-Inca diets reconstructed from extracted bone collagen showed a similar diet for men and women, mainly quinoa and tubers, with some maize, implying beer was shared between men and women. When the Inca took over, maize consumption rose, but male diets were much richer in maize than those of women. The men were also eating more meat than the women. This maize increase clearly came from beer, which was consumed not by everyone, but by the men. Hastorf believes that this change reflects an altered situation, in which the men paid a *mit'a* tax in agricultural labor and military service, during which they were fed meat, maize and corn beer. *Mit'a* separated men from women physically, politically, and symbolically. The Sausa research provides a remarkable example of how detailed archaeological work can document changes in men's and women's positions in ancient societies.

Cutting-edge science is also revealing past gender distinctions, which would otherwise be impossible to visualize from artifacts alone. One such project concerns the Middle Bronze Age of southwestern Italy during the third millennium BC. The San Abbondio cemetery near Naples contained women proven to have grown up in a different area from that of all the other burials in the graveyard. We know this from the trace elements in their teeth enamel, linked to the geologic elements (such as the soil adhering to plants) consumed during the first ten to fifteen years of age. The women's differed significantly from that of the locals. This evidence has led some archaeologists to believe that Middle Bronze Age women married those from other areas, and would then be absorbed into new communities. This exogamy (marrying outside the group) may have had a powerful role in cultural change in the past, though we can only speculate as to the nature of these marriages or the degree of choice that the incoming women did or didn't have. Yet it can be observed that when women move into the men's home then we are probably seeing a patriarchy at work, in which women's autonomy is invariably rather more limited.

There is far more to gender than merely looking for evidence of men and women who behave in ways that we recognize as "male" or "female." That is a false premise, based on assumptions that gender relations are timeless and have never changed. One useful approach involves looking at gender identity differently—what do men or women have in common? These shared experiences are sometimes more important than differences. A great deal depends on our mindsets, on the archaeologist's ability to look back at the past without bias, and without an assumption that inequality has always been part of gender relations. The fact is that inequality on the basis of sex was never inevitable. As the feminist archaeologist Rosemary Joyce wisely remarked in 2008, it is not methodologies that make exploring past sexual relations or gender roles different. "It is in beginning the philosophical commitments that we share with other students of sex and gender to acknowledge that our own position in society and history influences how we understand the past, to respect human dignity, including the dignity of people unlike ourselves, and to combat attempts to maintain inequalities in the contemporary world in every way possible." Doing this makes the past a powerful resource, and using the past as a resource is something that archaeology can do with convincing authority.

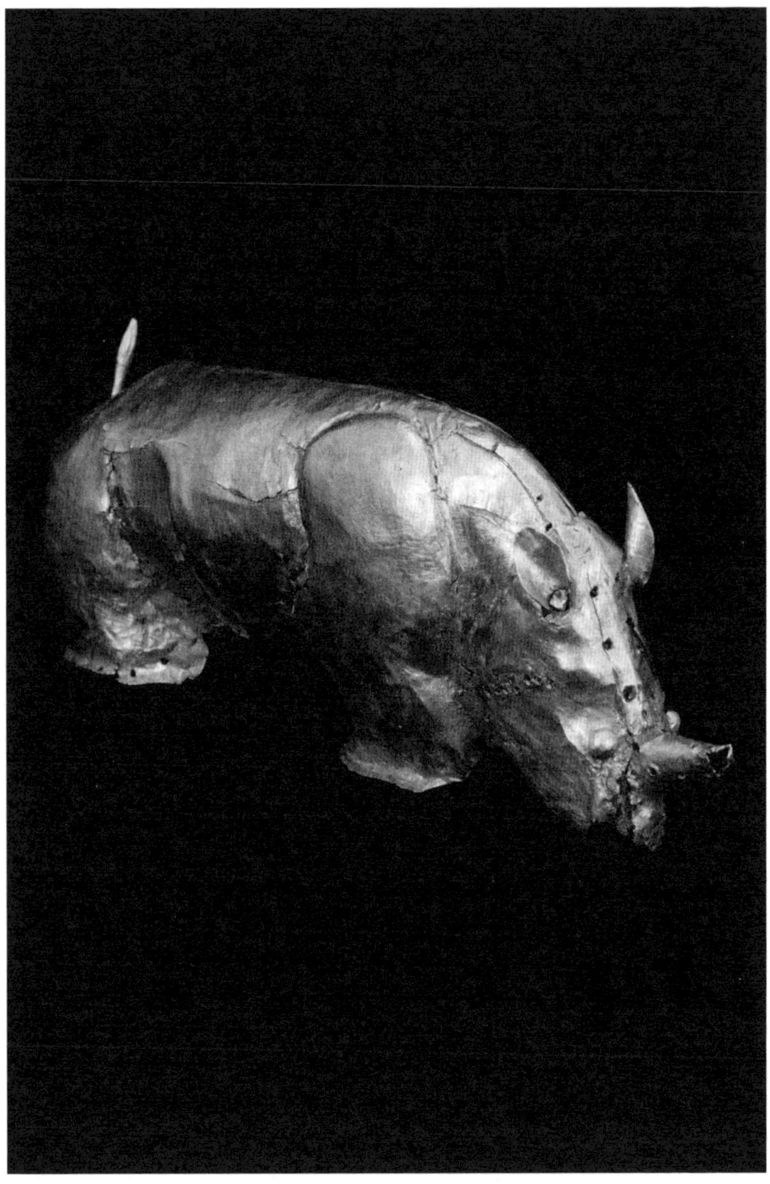

Figure 8. A rhinoceros modeled in gold sheet from Mapungubwe, Limpopo Valley, Southern Africa, *c.* AD 1250. This important African trading center was ignored in schoolbooks during the apartheid era to hide the fact black Africans had settled the area first.

5 Archaeology and Nationalism

Every nation has a past that makes it what it is. That past can be manipulated to justify its existence and its relationship to other nations. Inevitably, archaeology, like history, becomes involved in the agendas of politics, and its ideologies. The historian and Marxist Eric Hobsbawm once remarked that historians were to nationalism what poppy growers are to heroin addicts. "We supply the essential raw material for the market." Archaeologists do the same.

Despite its appetite for the past, nationalism is an entirely modern movement. Nationalism was invented—and invented is the correct word—in the seventeenth and eighteenth centuries, when the new Western European nation states reorganized and consolidated themselves. These nascent nation states defined themselves by clear borders, by far greater administrative intensity than traditional states, and by political autonomy and authority over their internal and external affairs. As the political scientist Anthony Giddens put it, modern nation states are "bordered power containers."

Before the eighteenth century, Europe was dominated by more flexible, multi-ethnic empires, such as the Russian empire, the Ottoman empire, and the Kingdom of Hungary, each of which contained many different groups of people, even if each empire was dominated by a particular one. At other times, there were smaller dynastic states, whose lands could easily be expanded through royal intermarriage, or merge with another state when the dynasties joined. Sometimes, too, very small territorial units existed, each with its own laws and own rulers—perhaps an abbot or a prince—but with no separate language or culture from those living around them.

But in the wake of the new European world order, each state sought to ensure the political coherence of its people. Each required a distinctive identity. This was—and is—based on the shared characteristics of its inhabitants, and generally comes from language, religion, politics, origin myths, and on ideas of a common ancestor. Indeed, the word "nation" comes from the Old French *nacion*, meaning "birth" or "place of origin." But the nation state's shallow roots must not be revealed: one of the chief paradigms of nationalism is primordialism, the idea that nationalism is a natural phenomenon and that nation states have always existed. By waving flags, evoking history, and telling stories, the nation created nationalism: its collective consciousness and its identity.

Little wonder, then, that archaeology more or less emerged hand in hand with the birth of the nation state. Just as anthropologists worry that they are the handmaidens of colonialism, so we might argue that archaeology has been a handmaiden—or certainly a tool—of nationalism. The original nation state builder, Napoleon, was a lover of archaeology. He often drew imagined parallels between France and the Roman empire: "I am a true Roman Emperor; I am of the best line of the Caesars—those who are founders," he said in 1812.

Today, the modern nation state is the predominant political form across the globe, with nationalism always at its core. As a consequence, many modern ideas about the past are permeated with nationalist ideologies. Very often invented national mythologies and mysticism are evoked by such ideas. Claims that the ancient Medes are direct ancestors of modern-day Kurds in Turkey and Iraq, or that the roots of Hindu nationalists lie four thousand years ago in the Indus civilization of present-day Pakistan (see Plate 8), cannot be supported by conventional scholarship, but this is irrelevant to the people who create such tales of the past. Similar stories are, of course, told in Europe and America.

Such accounts draw on the nation's imagined ancestral history, linking past peoples with modern-day cultural, "racial" groups on the basis of belief rather than science. Archaeologists take it as their responsibility to highlight and challenge examples of when the past is taken and warped to suit a political or religious agenda. For example, the celebrated myth of the Mound-Builders came into being during the nineteenth century, when scholars flatly believed that Native Americans in the North American Midwest were incapable of building large earthworks. To them, the mounds were the work of white conquerors from across the Atlantic. Archaeological survey and excavation of the mounds debunked this myth over a century ago.

A far more insidious attempt to rewrite history came from South Africa in the days of apartheid, from 1948 to the early 1990s. The white government, with its own nationalist agenda, claimed that black Africans only crossed the Limpopo river—the northern frontier that separates South Africa from Zimbabwe (then Rhodesia)—at the same time as Portuguese explorer Bartholomew Diaz landed at the Cape of Good Hope in AD 1488. This pronouncement appeared in school and university textbooks and was declared to be the historical truth. It just so happened that this narrative promoted the colonial picture that South Africa had been empty before Europeans arrived, which meant local Africans had no greater historical claim, or rights, over the region than the Europeans. Yet, all the while, the archaeology told a different story.

In the 1930s, archaeologists had been busy at the site of the ancient city of Mapungubwe, located in the Limpopo Province on the border between South Africa, Zimbabwe, and Botswana. There, they found important stone ruins, and a series of high-status graves containing considerable amounts of gold, most famously a golden rhino made from thin gold sheets (see Figure 8). At first, the "lost golden city of Mapungubwe" attracted widespread media attention, but soon the digs and discoveries, led by the University of Pretoria, were more or less kept secret. Mapungubwe provided uncomfortable evidence that black Africans had been living in the area centuries before any white colonists arrived at the Cape.

Mapungubwe was, in fact, the major focus of one of the largest known kingdoms in the African sub-continent. Peaking around AD 1200 to 1300, it was a complex, sophisticated, and class-based society, which lay at the edge of thriving international trading networks based on the monsoon winds that reached up to Egypt, over to India, and as far as China. It was only in 1994 that Mapungubwe's vibrant history became public knowledge. After the fall of apartheid, the golden rhinoceros was designated a national treasure in 1999.

The story of Mapungubwe is far from unique. Similar baseless arguments were applied to Great Zimbabwe (Chapter 3), north of the Limpopo river, after Rhodesia's Unilateral Declaration of Independence in 1965. In this case, the white government denied that the (largely) medieval center was of African origin and inspiration—despite generations of excavations dating back to 1905 that proved this. The official line in Rhodesia in the 1960s and 1970s was that the city was built by non-blacks. Paul Sinclair, one of the archaeologists working there at the time, recalled, "I was told by the then director of the Museums and Monuments organization to be extremely careful about talking to the press about the origins of the [Great] Zimbabwe state, that the government was pressurizing them to withhold the correct information. Censorship of guidebooks, museum displays, school textbooks, radio programs, newspapers, and films was a daily occurrence. Once a member of the museum board of trustees threatened me with losing my job if I said publicly that blacks had built Zimbabwe. He said it was okay to say the yellow people had built it, but I wasn't allowed to mention radiocarbon dates..." Fortunately, these racist exploitations of African history are now discredited.

For Paul Sinclair, the situation reminded him of the state of archaeology in Germany in the 1930s. Some of the most notorious nationalist research in the modern era was that of the late nineteenth and early twentieth centuries, such as that developed by the linguist and prehistorian Gustaf Kossinna. He believed that a well documented set of archaeological artifacts—a culture—was a sign of shared ethnicity. By equating prehistoric ceramic traditions with a unified ethnicity, he drew maps that showed supposed boundaries of the Germanic culture, which extended over nearly all of Europe. Kossinna's ideas were fervently adopted by the Nazi Party: here was the historical proof they needed to back their claims that the German nation had an ancient right to the lands they once occupied and to help justify their subsequent annexations of lands in Poland and Czechoslovakia.

Checking yet more boxes on the nationalist agenda, Kossinna also developed an origin myth for the Germans, based loosely on his linguistic work on Indo-European languages. It was he who introduced the idea of the Aryan race, presented as a "superior," "Nordic" people from a mythic Indo-Germanic homeland (hence Hitler's use of the Sanskrit swastika), who then expanded and influenced ancient Europe. The Aryan ideology became a terrible cornerstone of Nazi ideology. It allowed the barbaric treatment of all inherently "inferior" peoples (that is, anyone who wasn't Aryan) and provided the supposed proof that Germany ought to be the leading civilization in the world. Kossinna's doctrines ultimately paved the way for the death of millions of so-called *Untermenschen* ("sub-humans").

His ideas have, quite rightly, been long discredited as fictions that find zero support from the archaeological record. Moreover, since World War II, archaeology has become a global discipline, which, despite localized specialist research, ultimately transcends national boundaries. With its long-term, international perspective, archaeology now studies humanity as a single worldwide phenomenon, exploring how our species is different and similar, and the often illusory issues of identity, ethnicity, and race.

Slaying the Stereotypes

Archaeology, with its meticulous science-based approach, has the power to combat popular historical stereotypes and inventions. Among the most pervasive modern myths is that people belong to separate and clearly differentiated races that have deep and distinct roots. Racial classifications tend to be based on one's (or one's parents') country of origin, skin color, and general looks, from which are extrapolated certain character traits, notably in terms of intelligence and moral fortitude, or lack thereof. In 1994, Richard Herrnstein and Charles Murray wrote the widely selling book *The Bell Curve* in which they documented racial differences in IQ test scores, with the implicit assumptions that it was not only meaningful to classify people according to particular racial categories, but also that these races have different core characteristics (with certain races *naturally* more intelligent than others). Yet today's variations in skin color, often taken as the main badge of racial identity, have very shallow roots.

This point was demonstrated in 2017 when a DNA analysis of Britain's oldest complete skeleton, a fossil known as Cheddar Man, indicated that he had black skin, dark curly hair, and blue eyes (see Plate 9). Around 10,000 years ago, Cheddar Man was one of the earliest to cross from continental Europe to Britain at the end of the late Ice Age (across Doggerland, see Chapter 2). Scientists speculate that the light skin we see today can be traced to migrating farmers who mixed with and replaced populations in Britain as late as 4500 to 3500 BC—the first examples of the European blond hair mutation come from the Lake Baikal region of eastern Siberia around 17,000 years ago. As we moved out of Africa, most *Homo sapiens* would have retained their black skin for some time, with white skin being, in part, a response to the colder climate and the need for the skin to process more vitamin D from the sun. We can only imagine that this first black-skinned Briton was not exactly what the far-right white supremacist nationalist party, Britain First, must have envisaged "their" ancestor to look like.

Certainly these discoveries challenge the idea of long-standing and deep-rooted racial categories, and demonstrate the illusionary nature of our current racial categories. Not to be outsmarted by a bit of really ancient DNA, some nationalist groups in the UK and US prefer to focus on more recent times, suggesting that "the English" have a common Anglo-Saxon ancestry, which is based on biology. As a case in point, as 2017 shuddered to an end and the UK thrashed out its future in relation to the EU, the then leader of the UK Independence Party, Henry Bolton, fanned xenophobic flames by tartly stating that "in certain communities the indigenous Anglo-Saxon population is nowhere to be seen." But what is meant by this? No one living in fifth-, sixth- or seventh-century England would have identified him or herself as an Anglo-Saxon. Instead, this is a romanticized and heavily politicized identity that was promoted within nationalism. For it was only in the sixteenth century that pre-Norman people were consistently described as Anglo-Saxons, and it was only in the nineteenth century that this identity gained popularity, particularly under Queen Victoria and her (Saxon) husband.

Indeed, a recent DNA analysis of four skeletons from the Oakington Anglo-Saxon cemetery in Cambridgeshire shows a mixed heritage of Dutch, Danish, Welsh, Scottish, and local connections. Yet the grave goods indicate that people didn't base their cultural identity on any particular biological legacy. Rather, there is a genetic and cultural mix that reflects the long-term migratory ebb and flow of people.

Contrary to the ex-UKIP leader's claim, all modern white English people are not biologically descended from one discrete group of "Anglo Saxons," but from many groups, among them the Vikings, once England's most feared enemies. Or, at least, generations of authors, film-makers, and, indeed, scholars have tended to portray the Vikings as hated, ferocious, rapacious warriors set on conquest and wealth, who emerged from their Scandinavian fjords on bold voyages of discovery and adventure. This narrative, too, is both misleading and, simply, wrong. The Vikings badly need to be re-presented in a more accurate manner, using a range of sources that take into account such variables as gender, identity, and religion, ritual, and magic.

In 2016, the Swedish Research Council funded a ten-year project known as The Viking Phenomenon to achieve a closer understanding of the social processes of the Viking Age. The multidisciplinary project will examine a critical period in European history that had truly global implications. It will do so by examining the impact of the Vikings on other societies of the day. Among other things, the researchers are exploring the complex origins of the Viking Age. The heart of the project revolves around the hilltop cemetery and boat graves of Valsgärde in Sweden's Uppland, where people buried their dead for more than 400 years. The more than eighty Valsgärde graves, with their broad array of artifacts and imports, provide a magnificent opportunity to examine the gradual social changes that led to the Viking Age. Part of the project will revolve around other, far-flung sites, among them the spectacular Salme ship burials of about AD 750, the remains of a Scandinavian raiding party in Estonia on the other side of the Baltic Sea. Strontium isotopes of the bodies' teeth are providing priceless information of the origins of the attackers, and have shown that they may well have come from Valsgärde. This provides information of the broad-ranging activities of Norse raiders.

Economic inquiries underpin much of the research, including a study of raiding, which must have been a prime cause of many social changes that ensued. New investigations are revealing the active roles of women in Viking colonial missions, the importance of slavery and slaving to the fabric of Viking life, and more about army life on the move and piracy. The researchers will make use of historical archaeology from other areas such as the Caribbean and the Pacific, with their evidence of seafaring and colonization, to discover new ways of looking at the Viking past.

Beyond "Them and Us"

We've observed how nation states require a shared past for their people, so it should come as little surprise that exploited and dominated countries were often denied theirs. To many people in the West, even in these increasingly global and multicultural days, a region's history still begins with European contact—in South America with Hernán Cortés and his conquistadors as they gazed on Tenochtitlán, the stupendous capital of the Aztecs, in 1519; in the United States, perhaps a mention will be given to Norse landings on the North American continent but, ultimately, history is considered to have begun in truth when the Pilgrim Fathers landed at Plymouth Rock in 1620; in Central Africa, most history books of the 1950s began with the statement that, in 1855, the missionary explorer David Livingstone "discovered" the

Victoria Falls and the peoples of the far African interior; even half a century ago, most history curricula in Britain started with William the Conqueror and his invasion of England in 1066.

Still today, many of us tend to think of a history of "us" and a history of "them." Of course, there were notable exceptions to this prevailing view during the nineteenth century. In America, such anthropologists as Franz Boas and Frank Cushing, among others, as well as such sober students of the past as Samuel Haven of the American Antiquarian Society, believed as long ago as 1856 that Native Americans had occupied, and flourished, in their homeland for thousands of years. But these are exceptions, and a colonial, European-influenced perspective persisted.

Now, however, a thriving approach to the past, known collectively as indigenous archaeology, works to develop active and meaningful collaborative relationships with archaeologists, on the one side, descent groups and local communities on the other, as a way to build a more inclusive past. These collaborations can begin at the very first proposal of a project, and last through to the conservation and sharing of archaeological findings and beyond. This approach is commonplace in former colonies whose indigenous histories were once ignored, dismissed, hijacked, or completely misinterpreted by westerners. There are many examples of such projects, especially in the Americas, Australia, and Africa.

One is the Chocolá Archaeological Project in Guatemala, which involves excavations of an ancient Maya city occupied between 1000 BC and AD 200 before the peak of Maya civilization. A traditional archaeological attitude to the Maya was that the society collapsed and vanished (see Chapter 2) but, in fact—despite the genocides of the Guatemalan Civil War of 1960 to 1996—an estimated six million Maya, with their distinct cultural and linguistic heritage, still live throughout Mexico, Guatemala, Belize, El Salvador, and Honduras. The Chocolá Project works alongside the local Maya community, and seeks to integrate local knowledge, perspectives, history, and ideas into what is otherwise a science-based study of ancient Maya culture. Rather than charging into the area and taking away the archaeological finds, or even building a park for the enjoyment of western tourists, the team has community development and uncovering the past for the benefit of the locals at its core.

Enormous, and still insufficiently studied, archives of oral tradition that early anthropologists collected in North America await close study. Despite all these efforts, and the devoted research of generations of archaeologists through the late nineteenth and early twentieth centuries, it is only very recently that archaeology and anthropology have been drawn into the broad outlines of American history, very often under the rubric of Native American studies.

Indigenous archaeology first developed in Australia, tracing the cultures of the ancestors of the Australian Aborigines who settled there during the late Ice Age. They arrived by canoe and raft, island hopping at a time of much lower sea levels. These events, still relatively poorly understood, mark the beginnings of Australian history, not the explorations of Captain James Cook and the establishment of convict settlements.

It is only recently that Australian archaeologists have looked more closely at the long occupation of the continent prior to European influence, and set aside a long-held assumption that Aboriginal society remained virtually unchanged for tens of thousands of years. Yet with a post-colonial legacy of oppression, it is no coincidence that the indigenous people themselves have developed a deep suspicion and often resentment of archaeologists and their history making. This is now beginning to change, however, with notable examples of positive relationships becoming more commonplace. For instance, in 2017, new excavations at the richly painted Madjedbebe rock shelter near Kakadu National Park were conducted under a landmark agreement between the researchers and its traditional Aboriginal owners, who were given the right to veto the excavation at any time, had control over the artifacts, and had a final say over the findings announced. Working with a spirit of cooperation and respect, the results have been formidable, with sophisticated dating of the shelter's sediment indicating that people had reached Australia by 65,000 years ago, over 15,000 years earlier than previously thought.

Urban Identities

In urban settings, many citizens also strive to develop their own identities, and again the past is used to help with the narrative. Some of these supposed historical identities are again the fictions of nationalism. Even a single city can provide a wealth of examples. In AD 60, Boadicea of the Iceni tribe rose in rebellion against the Roman incomers. Her bloody revolt ended in defeat and she took poison to avoid falling into Roman hands. She became a revered folk hero over the centuries and was firmly linked with Londinium, the

Roman name for London, despite the fact that there is no clear archaeological evidence for her existence. In 1902, the statue *Boadicea and Her Daughters* was prominently erected by Westminster Bridge, near the Houses of Parliament, London. A legend was drawn upon to create a fabricated past that formed an image for the sculptor. It is archaeology that can examine such claims, while also uncovering new, and sometimes unexpected, dimensions to the past, at times incompatible with the vicissitudes of nationalism.

One of the largest recent urban excavation ventures is London's enormous Crossrail project, which bisects the sprawling city with a new subway line, and has revealed much unexpected history in vivid detail. In what is understood to have been the UK's biggest ever dig, archaeologists worked on over forty construction sites and uncovered over 10,000 artifacts. From an 8,000 year-old microlith (a tiny stone tool) to a 1990s rave poster found in a Crosse and Blackwell factory, the project revealed a wide slice of the history of London life.

Most sites were deeply buried and would not otherwise have been investigated were it not for the new tunnel. Among the digs was that at Spital Croft, an emergency cemetery for plague victims, situated just outside the location of the medieval walls of the City of London. Contemporary written accounts tell us that by the summer, or perhaps autumn, of 1348, plague had reached England; two years later, up to one half of London's population had succumbed to the infection. Spital Croft cemetery, a piece of land leased from nearby St Bartholomew's Hospital, was created in response to this catastrophe.

Very few of London's Black Death burial grounds have ever been excavated, so the results of the new work were impatiently awaited. The excavation revealed twenty-five skeletons, of which twenty-three were adults. When their teeth were subjected to stable isotope analysis, scientists found that most were not native Londoners. Instead, many had grown up in southern or eastern England with a few coming from much farther—including Scotland and the north of England. What surprised the team was how most of the dead were buried in single plots, and not dumped in a mass burial, as was previously assumed to be the case. The discrete plots demonstrated how there was sufficient time and care given to the dead, despite the unfolding catastrophe and the non-local origin of most of the victims. Digs like this give a very human face to the past and challenge our preconceptions and biases about past cultural practices.

For all the political ideologies that divide us, we are all stakeholders in the past. Our investments lie in the minute details of a suburban neighborhood or a cemetery of plague victims, or of a long-forgotten disaster, which can inspire a special, sometimes passionate, and sometimes very personal, interest in what we unearth. But there's another point that we often miss, and of which archaeology reminds us. All of us, wherever we live, are participants in the story of the human past. This common past is part of all of us, and offers precedents, warnings, and unexpected insights into our behavior. Above all, it reminds us that we are all *Homo sapiens*. What we have learned and what we share as members of the same species is far more important than the narrow, and often biased, perspectives that come down to us when we allow our understanding of ancient times to be perverted by political agendas, racist or religious doctrines, or outmoded ideologies.

Against the fabricated pasts, which are endlessly conjured by nationalism to uphold the legitimacy of the present order, archaeology is perhaps the most powerful tool of all. Though archaeologists—in this sense, like all scientists—may bring their own interpretive biases to the data, archaeology has the power to examine the past as dispassionately as possible. In this way, it sheds light on forgotten, inconvenient, misinterpreted, or denied pasts.

Figure 9. Tourists jam Curetes Street and the Library of Celsus, Ephesus, Turkey in 2011. The Library of Celsus was built between AD 114 and 117 by the son of Roman senator Tiberius Julius Celsus Polemaenanus. Ephesus was a Greek city, famous for its Temple of Artemis, one of the Seven Wonders of the Ancient World. The city flourished under the Romans after 129 BC.

6 The Tourist Effect

In the middle of the South Pacific, the great statues (*moai*) stand silent, facing inward on the island of Rapa Nui. Up to 32 feet (9.8 meters) high, their deep-set eyes gaze toward their ancestral lands. They are sculptures of revered, proud individuals with beetling brows, elongated ears, sloping noses, and closed, pursed lips. Some bear chieftain's topknots made of red lava, replicas of their hairstyles in life; others have shell eyes. All of them are thought to be images of deified ancestors (see Plate 10). Eight hundred and eighty-seven *moai* are known, carved between about AD 1200 and 1680, many of them still lying unfinished in the quarries in which they were carved. As the sun sets, the great statues cast long shadows over the land, a silent reminder of the power of the ancestors. Looking at them in the evening, they still appear to be watching over the land.

Rapa Nui, or Easter Island, receives around 50,000 and 80,000 visitors per year—more than eleven times the total population of the island. This tourism, largely driven by the island's archaeological heritage, is Rapa Nui's biggest industry. Generating a total annual income of US$46,000,000–90,000,000, the money has certainly helped to improve the standard of living for the locals. The island is tiny, however—just 15.5 miles, or 25 kilometers, from coast to coast—and struggles to cope with the vast numbers of tourists, especially their impact on the natural environment, with their waste alone amounting to about 20 tons a day. The government has responded by placing restrictions on the number of visitors per day and limiting the length of time tourists can stay. Whether this will have a positive effect remains to be seen.

Without doubt, archaeological sites can be major travel destinations and key contributors to national economies. One could look at the tourism and economic statistics of famous archaeological sites and state that archaeology matters because the public enjoys archaeology. But the picture is more complicated; certainly archaeological sites attract tourists and their wallets, but where does that money go? Whose past is being presented? And can archaeological sites and their environments survive the mass attention? Archaeology is important not only because it offers attractive destinations for the public, but also because archaeologists work to negotiate the important balance between engaging the public and protecting cultural heritage.

The Tourist Trail

Human heritage survives in many guises. Some locations commemorate the burial place of a pharaoh with a huge pyramid (see Plate 11), others are ruins such as Delphi in Greece, or the great caravan junction at Petra in Jordan, or a fortified city such as Chang'an in China. The world's cultural heritage is an important legacy, but the damage wrought to it over the centuries and millennia is catastrophic. Nonetheless, it is a miracle just how much has survived, either through being left undisturbed, or through deliberate conservation that attempts to mitigate the impact of all kinds of twenty-first century (and earlier) activities, from agriculture and deep plowing to mining, road construction, urban expansion, warfare, and the nefarious ravages of looters.

The term cultural heritage tends to cover a broad spectrum of human experience, including our built environment (from living townscapes to archaeological remains), natural environment (rural landscapes to agricultural heritage), and our historical artifacts (written documents to art). Although archaeological heritage goes far back in time, most sites on the tourist trail tend to date to the past 5,000 years.

China, for example, has become deeply involved in cultural heritage and cultural tourism, because the government sees its nation's past both as a powerful political tool, and as a source of valuable tourist income. Emperor Shi Huangdi's Terracotta Army is a case in point. This is an extraordinary discovery that will continue to involve teams of experts for decades. Thus far, archaeologists have uncovered some 8,000 terracotta soldiers and 130 chariots, dating to the third century BC, which are part of a large necropolis that surrounds the tomb of the first emperor of China. What is not generally realized is that most of the soldiers were excavated in fragments. In order to create a sufficiently stimulating visitor experience, the figures have been meticulously reassembled, and erected in their original ranks, so that tourists can gaze down upon the entire army. Visitors to the nearby museum can see technicians busy at work on the figures that are still fragmentary, piecing them together or perhaps reconstructing the paint with which they were once decorated. The soldiers, each with individual expressions, gaze into the distance, ever watchful. According to historical accounts, they were fierce, unrelenting warriors at close quarters with their leaders mounted on chariots.

Over one million tourists pass through the army's hangar-like display every year, a site so lucrative that it has profoundly affected the economy of nearby Xi'an. For visitors, the power of the emperor, and of history, comes alive, but it is the size of the regiment and the extraordinary efforts being made to preserve the elite detachment in perpetuity that stick in our minds. Shi Huangdi's regiment is a pinnacle of cultural heritage. It would be fascinating to visit once again a century from now. Perhaps, by then, archaeologists will have excavated the first emperor's tomb, thought to include a vault of stars, and a reproduction of the empire, complete with depictions of the Yangtze and Yellow rivers in mercury. There are indeed pressures to excavate, for there are dreams of a sharp rise in money-spending visitors. So far, the archaeologists have persuaded the authorities that they, and archaeologists everywhere, currently lack the technical expertise to do so. Here, as elsewhere, there is a delicate balance between the need to reach out and educate and the wish for income.

While attracting and engaging the public in the human past, there is a major downside to cultural tourism, which profoundly worries archaeologists who are responsible for conserving, maintaining, and monitoring such sites as Pueblo Bonito in Chaco Canyon, New Mexico, or the Avebury circles in southern Britain (see Plate 12). Quite simply, tourists are loving the past to death. At many sites, visitor counts reach dangerous numbers that threaten efforts to conserve the archaeology sustainably (see Figure 9).

There are tragic examples of serious tourist-related damage from all parts of the world. The Egyptian government generates major revenue from its ancient historical sites, between 12 and 13 percent of its GDP. But the amount the Egyptian government can afford to spend on conservation is lamentably small, often relying on international bodies such as UNESCO.

Many of the pharaohs' tombs in the Valley of the Kings in Upper Egypt are so affected with sweat from crowds of visitors filing through their narrow passages that you can literally see the paint peeling off the carved and decorated walls. Likewise, cave paintings in caverns such as Altamira in Spain and Lascaux in southwestern France are much faded and have had mold problems since their discovery, due to similar human pollution. Elsewhere, modern graffiti obscures ancient rock engravings in California, while art of the San people on South African rock shelter walls—dating to the past 3,000 years or more—is endangered by neglect and a lack of funds for protective fencing. Humans' very presence, our breath and perspiration, as well as footprints, are creating long-term problems. The insatiable appetite of mass tourism has swallowed many archaeological sites, even in more remote places.

The crisis is global. An average of two million visitors admire Angkor Wat in Cambodia per year. Crowds walk through narrow corridors and up ancient stairways that are eroding under their feet. One solution offered by the authorities is to divert visitors to lesser-known sites in the complex, such as the Khmer temple at Ta Prohm near Angkor Wat, which has magnificent bas-reliefs and the added (photographic) attraction of serpentine tree roots enfolding, and slowly strangling, its buildings (see Plate 13). Ta Prohm is quiet, the crowds are much smaller, but the problem is that everyone wants to visit Angkor Wat or nearby Angkor Thom, the most spectacular sites, which are on many an archaeological traveler's bucket list.

The damage to these sites is often not obvious and usually seen only in the long-term, especially on fragile rock or tomb paintings. As these fade, what can archaeologists do to preserve them? One solution, brilliantly executed at the Altamira and Lascaux rock art sites, is to build precise replicas nearby and close the originals to visitors. This has worked exceptionally well, and visitors can get up close to the art in ways that they could not were they in the caves themselves. But their reproduction, even though it brings income, has been very expensive: the latest reproduction of Lascaux, which opened in 2016, cost US$70,000,000 to build over six years.

One of the few painted prehistoric caves in France still accessible to the public is Niaux Cave, although it is only open three months of the year, and then only to twenty people at a time, eleven times a day. This is a tempo of tourism that allows the climate of the cave to recover. On this basis, a restricted few can step into Niaux Cave's main painted chamber, the Salon Noir, which is 66 feet (20 meters) across. In doing so, the visitor is transported over 12,000 years into the past. Six unevenly distributed panels on the walls display black-painted bison, wild horses, and ibex (mountain goats) standing motionless in the quivering light. The bisons' horns stand upright or lowered, their black manes bristle, tails hang limply, and legs are straight. It is as if the artist has stood above recently killed animals and sketched them where they lay (see Plate 14).

In Italy, the excavated remains at Pompeii are only now being conserved systematically by the Great Pompeii Project. Fortunately, nearby Herculaneum has been placed on a sustainable basis that balances excavation, preservation, and tourism, at a cost of some €20,000,000 (US$23,500,000), so there is hope for the future for the two Roman towns. This leads us to another issue: back in the early 1900s the longevity of ancient ruins was not a common concern for archaeologists. Much of the emphasis in archaeological circles was on discovery, excavation, and research. This is all still crucial to building a clearer picture of the past, but the archaeological record is being destroyed and eroded all around us and appears to have been a lower priority than research. It is only in recent years that heritage conservation has become a major concern for archaeologists, much of it under the rubric of cultural resource management. The field involves a difficult balancing act between adding to world culture by exposing the public to these sites, and contributing to national economies, while also ensuring the longevity of these unique locations. How should we manage these sites, and can the public enjoy their past without destroying the record of it?

Save Our Sites

The rather unappealing and corporate sounding cultural resource management (CRM) aims to be a force for good as the dominant archaeological activity in North America, and appears under various names in Australia, Japan, and the United Kingdom. CRM and its equivalents have been around for decades, beginning with surveys before World War II that examined river basins throughout North America that were affected by Army Corps of Engineers projects and other hydrological operations. With abundant fish, game, mollusks, and waterfowl, many of these basins were favorable places for people to settle and were rich in archaeological sites as a result. The Glen Canyon Dam in Utah, built between 1956 and 1966, formed Lake Powell. The areas to be flooded were the subject of an archaeological survey that located over 200 sites that were under threat. Monitoring of the sites that were not flooded still continues under the aegis of the National Park Service. An equivalent effort in Britain is a charitable trust called RESCUE, widely known for its logo—a drawing of Stonehenge in a bulldozer bucket. Since the 1960s, CRM has become an international business, engaged in projects of all kinds, ranging from investigations of single sites to city blocks, entire watersheds, and even larger areas.

CRM, wherever it is carried out, is, ultimately, in the mitigation business. It takes measures to minimize damage to archaeological sites, be they a scatter of stone tools or pot fragments, an early agricultural village, or a place sacred to the local communities. The boundaries of a CRM project are usually closely defined, which places a limitation on any excavations carried out on sites within the defined area. Mitigation takes many forms, from carefully excavating and recording a site that is due to be destroyed by building work, to total excavation, which destroys the site, but is recorded for posterity with the finds being preserved. In many cases, archaeologists and other stakeholders, such as local residents, campaign to save a site by changing the development's footprint. Slightly re-routing a road or moving proposed buildings a short distance are often viable solutions. When faced with a site that is under threat, the question to be answered is ultimately a simple one: are there artifacts, structures, burials, or other remains within the project area that need to be conserved by some form of mitigation strategy? Such decisions are informed by all kinds of legislation, by the site's importance, tribal laws, and other regulations, which vary greatly from place to place and country to country.

Nearly everywhere in the world, both isolated finds and entire archaeological sites are the property of the state. This is not so in the United States, where private ownership of land is vested in the constitution. Under these circumstances, any site on privately owned land is the property of the owner. Responsibility for mitigating the impacts of modern development are entirely the responsibility of the landowner. They are the stakeholders of record, even of land historically owned by a now-displaced indigenous group. Fortunately, many landowners take their responsibilities seriously.

Regrettably, others do not, following the example of early landowners who sold their sites and their contents for profit and development—as when

British colonialists took almost all of the bricks of the great third millennium BC Indus civilization city of Harappa (located in today's Pakistan) for reuse as ballast for nearby rail lines. Though such extreme examples rarely happen today, without strict laws in place the past remains open to destruction. Yet even where such laws exist, the past may still fall foul of industrial development, which sometimes takes priority. Such was the case when the grand Church of St Lambertus in Immerath, Germany, was demolished in 2018 to make way for a surface coal mine, despite its inclusion on the formal list of Germany's heritage monuments since 1985. This imposing church had been built in 1888, replacing one that had existed in the twelfth century. The church was demolished despite protests, and its burials moved.

Pre-excavation mitigation—that is, identifying the site's archaeological potential, usually through desk-based assessments, geophysical surveys, or trial excavations before any development takes place—is a useful form of protection, which requires careful and, sometimes, agonizing decisions. On the whole, recent generations of archaeologists have done a good job of encouraging mitigation. In some countries such as the UK, it is written into law.

Conservation of the past is something very different: it is a permanent decision to preserve a site or archaeological finds in perpetuity for future generations. Many people imagine that conservation is something that happens only in laboratories or museums. Ideally, it should begin at the moment an artifact, animal bones, or structure emerges from the soil. Destructive processes such as damp, insect damage, or mold have to be checked at once, and the find stabilized. Some discoveries are unique and receive immediate conservation. Howard Carter took eight years to clear Tutankhamun's tomb, much of the time spent stabilizing such finds as the king's golden mask and throne so they could be moved to a museum. Leonard Woolley, who excavated the 4,800 year-old Royal Burials at Ur in southern Iraq, recovered a gold-inlaid standing ram, part of an offering stand, from a royal burial at Ur by pouring plaster-of-Paris into holes in the surrounding clay in the early 1930s. But humbler finds, especially of perishable materials like cloth or wood, require conservation from the moment they are unearthed if they are to survive. Preserving one's discoveries, whether prosaic or spectacular, is one major responsibility for excavators.

Conservation has become a highly specialized process, which relies heavily on hi-tech science, especially when conserving grave goods and delicate fabrics.

But there is much more to conservation than just the unique discoveries, much as we admire them. The finds and food remains from even modest excavations fill numerous bags, envelopes, and boxes. CRM has become such a vast enterprise that a shortage of repositories for all kinds of finds, from stone tools and potsherds to cattle bones, glass beads, and statuary is assuming crisis proportions in many countries. Where are we going to store these records of the past on a permanent basis? Such humble finds as stone tools may seem disposable, especially if they come from an obscure site, but who knows what advances in archaeology may make them a prized source of information in the future?

Conservation means preserving our cultural heritage for the long-term future, and also reporting one's finds in a comprehensive, thorough way, even if this record is only digital. The number of unpublished archaeological excavations around the world, many by well-known archaeologists, is one of the inconspicuous scandals of archaeology. If archaeologists don't put their excavations and surveys on record, who will? It is no coincidence that much contemporary archaeological research takes place in air-conditioned laboratories, not in the field. Researchers are trying to tease fresh information from old, often unpublished, excavations. An essential part of all this activity is what is now known as public archaeology, which is concerned with outreach, stewardship, stakeholders, and heritage preservation.

Public Archaeology

Archaeology has a duty not only to conserve the past, but also to present it. Yet while the story of tourism may suggest the two are in opposition, many argue that if archaeology involves the public in their shared past, this can help improve the chance of its preservation.

Public archaeology has many faces. The most visible are TV series, radio programs, and mass-market books, as well as popular journals. These outlets are enormously valuable, and topics can cover everything from human beginnings to Maya civilization, Roman warfare to the archaeology of the industrial revolution, or even digging through modern garbage. Many archaeologists have appeared in or served as consultants on TV series.

In terms of writing, the range of topics for general consumption is open-ended. Some subjects that have recently crossed our own desks are what to wear when on a tour of ancient Egypt, the qualities of Howard Carter and how they relate to a successful CEO's strategies, and the archaeology of the world's earliest beds. Increasingly, however, non-fiction works on archaeology revolve around pressing issues such as climate change and its impact on ancient and modern societies, the reasons why civilizations collapsed, and discussions derived from multidisciplinary inquiry that reflect the approach of many archaeologists today. Websites, blogs, and social media are fertile avenues for disseminating archaeology to thousands of people, but with these outlets, as well as every other one, everything depends on the narrative. This should be an area where archaeology excels, given the extraordinary diversity and fascination of its subject matter. Archaeologists are in the position to be consummate storytellers, but it can be difficult not to be consumed with the narrow fascination of one's own work. When that happens, we risk forgetting the broader potential of a well-told story for raising awareness. Public archaeology is, in the final analysis, an avenue for storytelling about the past, the present, and the future.

Whose Past?

In presenting the past to the public, it is important to ask whose past are we showing, and are we in the best place to be able to show it? (See Chapters 3 and 5 for how archaeology is confronting its colonial roots and collaborating with local and descent communities.) This is particularly contentious when dealing with human remains.

The treatment and repatriation of human remains has been a burning issue in many countries whose indigenous peoples have demanded the reburial of skeletal remains excavated or looted from cemeteries and prehistoric settlements since the nineteenth century. At least 650,000 humans lie in US museum collections—the exact number is uncertain. Native Americans have been vociferous in their protests, and with good reason. Many Indian communities are incensed by burial excavation and have lobbied for laws that forbid such activity altogether. A growing public awareness of the issues involved led to the passage of the Native American Grave Protection and Repatriation Act (NAGPRA) in 1990. This obliges all federal agencies and museums to inventory their human remains and funerary objects. If their research establishes a linear relationship between ancient human remains and living people, the act requires the organization holding them to notify the descendants and offer to repatriate them.

Controversy still surrounds NAGPRA, sometimes pitting archaeologists who want to study skeletons found in excavations with the latest medical technology against Native American groups. While such issues are far from resolved, NAGPRA has resulted in much more routine consultation between tribal councils and local communities, the actual stakeholders in local history.

The same concerns have been voiced by Australian Aborigines, who have striven for strict control of excavations, especially on prehistoric sites. A broad-ranging agreement drafted by the World Archaeological Congress in 1989, the so-called Vermillion Accord, named after a South Dakota city, calls for respect both for the dead and for the wishes of their descendants, as well as for the scientific research value of human remains. It established the principle that mutual consideration between different stakeholders, including scientists, should balance the needs of education and science against the correct, respectful burial of ancestors. Such a two-way understanding is slowly taking hold.

In British Columbia, the Kunghit Haida village known as SGang Gwaay Llanagaay ("Red Cod Island"), commonly called Ninstints today, lies on Anthony Island, part of the Haida Gwaii archipelago. In its heyday in the early to mid-nineteenth century, the settlement was a forest of totem and mortuary poles set before at least twenty long houses at the back of a small tidal bay with a sandy beach. Ninstints was largely abandoned after a smallpox epidemic in 1862. Many of the magnificent totem poles still stand and have been the subject of ardent controversy (see Figure 10).

Ninstints is a deeply emotive place: silent, remote, and heavily overgrown. Many of the poles were removed to the Royal British Columbia Museum and other institutions before Haida wishes were respected and the remaining ones left in place to decay back into the forest. The great totems, many of them masterpieces of Haida carving, depict ravens and mythic beasts. Moss grows on the cedar; green shoots sprout from many of them. Some poles are leaning, close to falling. This is an important place for their descendants, the stakeholders who still live on Haida Gwaii. Both the Canadian government and the Haida manage Ninstints through the Archipelago Management Board, comprising representatives from each group. They determine all operational, planning, and management actions. The hereditary leaders of the Haida have moral authority over the site and other ancient Haida settlements. Their advice is at the center of conservation solutions, which revolve around the potential impacts of climate change, wind, humidity, temperature, marine pollution,

Figure 10. Totem poles at the nineteenth-century Haida village of Ninstints on Anthony Island, Haida Gwaii, Canada. After many of the poles were removed, the Haida had to request that their preference for the poles to remain as they are be respected.

and tourism, as well as recreational activities nearby—to mention but a few of the potential issues. The emphasis is on the long-term preservation of the site for future generations.

Cultural heritage is universal. It is much more than a single site, such as Ireland's Newgrange burial mound, or even an entire abandoned city such as Amarna or Naucratis in Egypt. It is not simply an interest in recording or protecting the material culture of a site such as Teotihuacán or colonial Jamestown; it also extends to cultural or sometimes sacred places in the widest sense of the world. Different people, groups, and societies have profoundly diverse perspectives on the past and on what archaeology means to them. The Hopi and other southwestern Native American tribes, for example, spend a great deal of time on the preservation of sacred places mentioned in oral tradition, some of them identifiable physical locations, others intensely sacred spots that are virtually invisible unless one knows what to look for. When archaeologists work to present and preserve the past for the public, it is important to remember who is included, who runs the risk of being excluded, and how a cultural heritage strategy can ensure an archaeological site offers a coherent, inclusive past that benefits everyone.

Figure 11. The ruins of the Temple of Bel at Palmyra, Syria, destroyed by Islamic State militants in 2015. Palmyra was a major caravan trade city under the Romans.

7 Protecting the Past

When, in 2001, a set of religious fanatics calling themselves the Taliban ("teachers") decided to destroy Afghanistan's divine Bamiyan Buddhas, the world looked on in horror. Described as a "national tragedy" by the country's post-Taliban leader, Hamid Karzai, the Buddhas had occupied their place in the Bamiyan valley since the sixth century AD. Hewn into a sandstone cliffside, the smaller Buddha stood at 115 feet (35 meters), the other at an extraordinary 174 feet (54 meters). Works of spiritual and artistic beauty, the Buddhas spoke of human connections through the compelling range of cultural influences in their distinctive Gandharan art style. This artistic melding is not surprising, for Bamiyan lies on the Silk Road, the old caravan route that linked East with West, from the markets of China to those of Rome and beyond. Great splendors dot the route, among them Palmyra, a site of deep antiquity that reached its apex around the third century AD, during the height of the Roman empire.

Replete with monumental architecture including a fine temple dedicated to the Babylonian god Bel and a Roman theatre, Palmyra remained well preserved—until 2015. During the Syrian civil war, the ancient city was taken by ISIL (Islamic State of Iraq and the Levant), who wrought destruction upon it, felling buildings and sabotaging artifacts (see Figure 11). Although both of these examples are ideologically linked, cultural vandalism is nothing new, and takes many forms.

From 1801 to 1812, Thomas Bruce, the 7th Earl of Elgin, employed agents to strip off the marble sculptures from the Parthenon (see Plate 16). He resorted to bribery to remove the sculptor Phidias' masterpieces from the temple, including 247 feet (75 meters) of the Parthenon frieze and fifteen metope panels depicting battles between the Lapiths and centaurs, which cost Elgin about £70,000 (about US$93,800) at today's exchange rate. He intended originally to use them to decorate his country house in Scotland, but a costly divorce suit forced him to sell them to the British government for £35,000 (about US$46,900), amid furious objections from many quarters, including the poet Lord Byron. The debate over the so-called Elgin Marbles has continued ever since, with the Greek government demanding their return. So far, they remain in London in the British Museum. Yet Greece has built a magnificent museum at the foot of the Acropolis, where both the remaining originals and plaster casts of the others are displayed, ready for when the marbles in London return to their homeland.

Today, illegal markets are still encouraging the removal of ancient material, and in some areas the archaeological record seems to be disappearing before our eyes. Thousands of artifacts vanished from the looted Iraq Museum in Baghdad during the US invasion in 2003, including its priceless collection of cuneiform tablets. These finds quietly appear on the international market, as have objects looted by ISIL on the grounds that they are "idolatrous." As we will see, archaeologists are involved in curbing this market, as well as addressing the actions of archaeologists from the colonial past.

Collecting Ethics

Although looting takes on many forms, the urge to collect ancient artifacts gained momentum with the rising popularity of the Grand Tour through classical lands during the eighteenth and early nineteenth centuries. Wealthy travellers returned home with Roman statuary and exhibited it in their country houses. The remarkable finds of Roman art from Herculaneum and Pompeii, conducted by mining engineers for the king of Naples after 1783, added a new frenzy to the lust to own the past. Meanwhile, less privileged landowners dug into burial mounds. This usually involved some hastily created trenches, followed by a fine dinner where one exhibited to one's friends the loot that had been found. On one occasion, in 1840, eight mounds in southern England were opened in just one afternoon.

The wish to display something ancient on the mantel, even something as small as a pot fragment, was perhaps inspired by the new European nationalistic emphasis on the importance of the past—although collecting probably also taps into a human desire to own exotica. Back in 1921, a French physician, Henri Codet, wrote a pioneering dissertation on collecting. There were, he said, four underlying motives: "The need to possess, the need for spontaneous activity, the impulse to self-advancement, the tendency to collect things." Another Frenchman added that collecting was, "not a pastime but a passion, and often so violent that it is inferior to love and ambition only in the pettiness of its aims." Today, people collect everything from antiquities to beer-bottle caps and even barbed wire, to say nothing of automobiles and Old Masters. It follows that everything has a market value and can be purchased, the value depending on the demand for a particular artifact and its rarity. Exactly where on an archaeological site the object was found or its scientific value has absolutely no relevance to the antiquities market. All that matters is the collectible itself. In some countries, tomb robbing is a technically illegal yet full-time profession. For example, *tombaroli* is a notorious Italian term for full-time, professional looters who concentrate on early Italian Etruscan tombs. Despite strenuous efforts at legislation in most parts of the world, illegal looting continues unabated.

By no means is everyone disturbing archaeological sites for profit. Many consider their searches for projectile points, potsherds, or coins a hobby. This is particularly true of metal-detector enthusiasts, many of whom comb American Civil War battlefields and other historical locations; they have often been the first to discover important burials or hoards, such as the so-called Staffordshire Hoard in the UK. This country has developed a Portable Antiquities Scheme, which sees archaeologists working closely with metal detectorists, many of whom are enthusiasts, unmotivated by economic gain. The two combined, with considerable success, to examine topsoil at locations that would be disturbed by deep plowing. The UK's 1996 Treasure Act, which safeguarded the rights of finders, gave them an incentive to come forward with their finds. Finds liaison officers visit local detector clubs regularly, identify and record finds, then return them to their discoverer. The exception to this returns policy is in finds of buried treasure, which are subject to UK state control.

The policy has worked well. In 2009, detectorist Terry Herbert unearthed the largest cache of Anglo-Saxon gold ever found in Britain, the aforementioned Staffordshire Hoard (see Figure 12). This yielded more than 3,500 pieces of gold and silver, mostly from weapons, including inlaid sword

Figure 12. Items from the Staffordshire Hoard. A huge conservation project followed the discovery.

hilts, dating to around the eighth century AD. The hoard may have been a sacrificial offering—no one knows. As required by law, an expert committee assessed the value of the find, at £3,200,000 (around US$4,000,000). The funds needed to buy them for the state was raised from the non-profit sector and, surprisingly, almost £900,000 (roughly US$1,300,000) from the public. The proceeds were split between the finder and the landowner, the finds between two museums.

Few detector finds are as spectacular as the Staffordshire Hoard, and while some information was lost during its hasty excavation, the Portable Antiquities Scheme has done much to raise awareness of the importance of reporting even small archaeological discoveries. But this is only a small part of concerted efforts by both official and international non-profit organizations to control and eliminate looting and undeclared finds. Antiquities departments in many countries, among them Egypt, Iraq, Mexico, and Peru, actively prosecute robbers, and attempt to protect major sites.

How does one respond to this wave of destruction? Many police departments maintain distinct units that specialize in art crimes, for the antiquities trade runs afoul of criminal legislation in many countries.

The New York Police Department has such a unit, as does the Metropolitan Police in London. China, Egypt, Italy, Mexico, and Peru are among the nations active in trying to control archaeological exports. One weapon is the so-called memorandum of understanding (MOU), where countries work together to control the importation of antiquities and coordinate efforts to control smuggling. Such efforts are valuable, but they operate at the destination, when the objects have already been plundered and have likely passed through many hands before being exported illegally.

Successful intervention of looted antiquities requires the policing of excavations, contact with such intermediaries as dealers and shippers and, at the end of the chain, mediation with the collector who makes the purchase, whether an individual or an institution. In recent years, efforts have begun to create a much more comprehensive approach that combines the knowledge and experience of individual stakeholders, from archaeologists and local communities, to the police and collectors. The Heritage Management Organization (HERITAGE), run out of the University of Kent in England, is attempting to coordinate such cooperative activity. It is a huge task, featuring satellite monitoring of sites and recognizing patterns of activity on the ground, as well as the involvement of local communities. Databases provide information on provenance of finds, and volunteers are trained to identify stolen objects. Ultimately, the most powerful weapon is public opinion, originating among local stakeholders, who may have violent objections to private ownership of important archaeological finds.

Another approach is through collectors, who are often seen as the enemy by archaeologists. Yet collectors can be ethical, cultured, and knowledgeable people, who are very careful when they make a purchase. Others simply do not know how to buy responsibly. High-level collectors tend to have valuable information on clandestine dealers and are familiar with the rigorous checking needed to verify the origins of truly important items. HERITAGE has taken an important step in Greece, where it recently organized the first meeting between collectors, the antiquities authorities, and the police. Such collaboration is invaluable, as strategies of close collaboration are often effective. But, crucially, all the relevant stakeholders have to come together for solutions with open minds—if they do, there's a chance that the illegal antiquities trade will become a phenomenon of the past. Yet no one involved has any illusions as to the difficulties of the task. The emotions behind collecting are powerful; the profits for dealers and also for poverty-stricken tomb robbers are a compelling incentive. The mechanisms for enforcement ultimately depend on profound convictions on the part of all involved that vandalism of the past is wrong.

It is, of course, both a local and an international problem. There is now a common acceptance by the global community that not only national and regional governments, but also the public, have a responsibility to preserve national heritage. This remit can be interpreted in many ways, but it is, in general, the notion that conservation and legislation are the foundations of such work.

A gradual shift in archaeological priorities is under way, with a quiet determination to rely as much as possible on non-intrusive methods such as ground-penetrating radar to keep excavation to a minimum and preserve heritage finds as far as is possible. Internationally, the World Heritage Convention of 1972 set up a committee that chooses sites for a World Heritage list that covers almost 800 natural and human-made sites. There is no money attached to the designation, but it acts as a spur to implement adequate conservation methods. There is also a World Heritage in Danger list, which covers threatened sites, among them Palmyra in Syria.

Originally, private collectors were thought of as respectable guardians and conservators of the past. Yet funding for today's depredations comes largely from unscrupulous collectors. The destruction to history is beyond imagination. One Italian tomb robber published his memoirs in the 1980s, in which he boasted of clearing, over three decades, about 4,000 Etruscan tombs dating to between the eighth and third centuries BC. He probably knew more about Etruscan tombs than anyone, but the loss to our knowledge of their burial customs and social life is irreparable. Similarly, the damage in the American Southwest is just as catastrophic and began in the late nineteenth century when collectors acquired mummified Native American burials preserved in dry caves and pueblos, as well as ancient basketry and spectacular painted pottery. Today's robbers work at night with two-way radios, police scanners, and lookouts. Entire cemeteries in Peru are so riddled with looters' potholes that they look like World War I battlegrounds.

Unfortunately, museums used to play a decisive role in all this, sometimes filling their cabinets with stolen items—whether from the hands of looters or, indeed, unscrupulous pre-twentieth-century archaeologists. Fortunately, many of the world's great museums will no longer accept gifts of antiquities that have been exported illegally from their countries of origin, and many work vigilantly against the trade in black market antiquities. There are notorious examples of how this used to happen, though, as in the case of the Euphronius Krater, acquired by the Metropolitan Museum of Fine Art in New York in 1972 for US$1,000,000 without researching its dubious ownership history. After a thirty-year dispute, it was returned to Italy in 2008. Case after case can be cited, almost all involving large sums of money. The question has to be asked: who owns the past? The answer is, of course, that we all do, and certainly the countries where artifacts originated, not only wealthy collectors or museums.

Looting and Protecting

We discussed the repatriation of human remains in Chapter 6, but there has also, in recent years, been an upsurge in demands that major museums in Europe, the United States, and elsewhere, return items taken during colonial-era excavations and research. These objects may be currently in the hands of national governments and can sometimes be traced to descent communities. When they were exported, often through agreements made between powerful private individuals, a common excuse was that conditions in many of the former colonies, from where most objects invariably came, did not provide a safe haven for archaeological finds. Wallis Budge, a notorious keeper at the British Museum a century ago, once remarked of mummies exported from Egypt, "every unprejudiced person who knows anything of the subject must admit that once a mummy has passed into the care of the trustees, and is lodged in the British Museum, it has a far better chance of being preserved there than it could possibly have in any tomb, royal or otherwise, in Egypt." Besides, he argued, it would receive far greater exposure in the Museum, where it was beyond the reach of evils, ancient or modern. He flattered himself that he had the moral right, thus looting sites was, in this case, presumably legitimate, whether along the Nile or when exporting clay tablets from Mesopotamian cities, in which he excelled. Today, the situation is radically different, making the legal export of antiquities much harder, or even impossible. Not that this prevents robbers or the illicit activities of dealers working in the shadows, for whom the money on offer is too tempting to ignore.

Preserving the past is an international, national, and local issue. People intimately involved in conservation and educating people about archaeology can be professional archaeologists or individuals from any walk of life. In recent years, much of the focus has been on local issues and stakeholders, whose active involvement in preservation issues result in a variety of outcomes, everything from saving threatened sites to ensuring that artifacts go to museums instead of private pockets. Since 1973, the city of Alexandria, Virginia, close to Washington DC, has fostered an active archaeology program, where the city's archaeologists, volunteers, and students work closely with residents and developers to study and manage sites unearthed within the city boundaries. These include ships sunk along the old waterfront and the Lee Street site, which is the focus of Alexandria Archaeology Museum. Local archaeologists uncovered a bakery, taverns, and residences that lay alongside the bustling waterfront. The same block became a hospital support facility for the Union Army during the American Civil War. The long-term program and museum opened up the city and the region's 13,000 year-old history to locals and visitors alike.

Another North American example comes from Tucson, Arizona, where an area of 4.3 acres (1.7 hectares) set out for a new courthouse was exposed down to bedrock during the preparation of the site for development, revealing occupation going back about 4,000 years. The excavations uncovered the large Alameda Stone historic cemetery. The dig and the 1,044 bodies recovered required consultations with a range of stakeholders, including Native American communities who wanted their graves left alone and Latin Americans, who welcomed the chance to learn more about their forebears. Pima County authorities spent US$1,000,000 on the reburial and repatriation project. This four-year project was conducted to the highest ethical and methodological standards. (In the end the dead had to be moved, but photography was forbidden.) They were reburied with respect and the excavation answered important historical questions about the city.

Meanwhile, in Peru, great strides are being taken to engage the community. This is a relatively poor country but one that is rich with archaeology. The temptation to loot is all around—something that started when the Spanish colonists invaded, after all. Indeed, in 1987, a group of local looters tunneled into the Huaca Rajada, a rain-weathered, mud-brick pyramid not far from the village of Sipán in the Lambayeque coastal region of northern Peru. Over the course of a few days, the band had extracted large numbers of valuable metal objects, destroying hundreds of ceramics and human remains in the process. High on their new bounty, the robbers fought, and one was shot dead. The murder drew the police, who realized what had happened. The chief of police immediately telephoned the local archaeologist, Walter Alva, and urged him to come to help secure the site, which was by now riddled with potholes and swarming with local villagers hoping to find more.

On a recent visit to Peru, we spoke with Alva's assistant archaeologist, Luis Chero, about his and Alva's work and the true personal horror of these early days. He recalled how, for the first six months, he and Alva were forced to hide in the looters' tunnels and hastily dug pits at night to protect the site, and how they feared for their lives from the locals who were angry that their treasure had been usurped. The great challenge, knew Alva and Chero, was to get the surrounding community on board. An early solution was to employ as many locals as possible on the site, to provide them with a legitimate source of income while also instilling a rightful pride in their past.

Since those early days, Alva's team has uncovered fourteen previously untouched tombs. Known collectively as the Lords of Sipán site, these extraordinarily rich tombs date from around AD 50 to 700, and rival any found in Egypt (see Plate 15). So much material was recovered that two world-class museums were created. Today, the Lords of Sipán museum complex attracts around 200,000 tourists a year, and the area is consequently economically much richer. Alva has wisely used money generated by the site to set up projects to benefit the local community, including everything from the installation of running water, to the construction of a new community center, as well as training locals in traditional crafts. As Chero told us, illicit robbing is no longer an issue in this corner of Peru: there is much more to live for.

Although not always so dramatic, community projects abound everywhere. In the UK, CITiZAN (or the Coastal and Intertidal Zone Archaeological Network) is a project that aims to monitor the seemingly relentless destruction of Britain's coastal and estuarine sites, most of which have no statutory protection. The project is enormous and encompasses all manner of locations, from eroding prehistoric forests to Roman forts and abandoned barges. Coordinated by archaeologists, it draws on armies of volunteers, usually from the nearby communities. Locals, as the archaeological team agrees, tend to know and care a great deal about their area, making them the ideal people to monitor the sites. The project has a strong ethical code in place, including the expectation that volunteers will immediately report any finds or human remains. In the face of economic cutbacks and a lack of funding, CITiZAN is a creative and commendable way of engaging people power to protect the past.

A great deal of community archaeology develops on a much smaller scale, especially projects that work closely with small groups of stakeholders, who have deep roots in their region. A private organization, the Archaeological Conservancy, acquires and protects archaeological sites in the United States, working closely with local stakeholders. The conservancy recently took over ownership of Amity pueblo in the upper Little Colorado region of northeastern Arizona. This is an intensely significant ancestral village for the Pueblo of Zuni, a rubble mound that may contain as many as sixty rooms. The pueblo lies in an area that connects Zuni pueblo and its inhabitants with the people's place of origin in the Grand Canyon. The action, taken in collaboration with federal and state agencies, the tribes, and the Arizona State Museum, among others, comes after years of neglect and destruction at the edge of the site. The conservancy proposes to develop a long-term management plan, consulting tribes, local property owners, and government agencies, which will include both monitoring the site and providing access to the land for the tribes, who regard this as a sacred place.

Talking History

Community archaeology takes many forms, including reconciling archaeological research with spoken traditions. The Zuni people of the American Southwest have occupied their homeland for over a thousand years. They reside in a cultural landscape with places named by them to symbolize and recall the remote past. This past is projected into the contemporary world by defining and understanding the landscape. Zuni traditional history and cultural geography are an independent source of historical information.

The Zuni have a rich body of well-recorded oral tradition, including their "from the beginning talks," which describe their emergence and subsequent migration to Zuni pueblo, the "Middle Place." *Telapnawe*, folktales or legends, which mainly revolve around the Zuni river valley, are often recited to teach the young. Among them are "prayer talks," which are chants or prayers recited during ceremonies. They are often repetitions of fixed formulae performed with gestures and oral elaborations. There are many such talks that begin with the emergence from the lower world and the search for the Middle

Place. Older men use various narratives to pass on the main outlines of Zuni history to the young in *kivas* on such occasions as the winter solstice. Other accounts are shared within families around the hearth during the winter.

These oral traditions are dynamic and ever-changing, but once they are written down, they inevitably become a more static view of history. From these spoken sources comes a summary that begins with primordial Zuni spirits emerging at a place named *Chimik'yana'kya dey'a*, deep in a canyon along the Colorado River. Divine instruction taught them all manner of prayers, rituals, and sacred talks before their emergence. Once in the world, and guided by their religious societies, they migrated to what is now the Little Colorado River. Along the way, they stopped and occupied villages for "four days and four nights," a symbolic expression of a longer, unspecified time. At one of the springs on their journey, they assumed the appearance of humans. In the Lower Colorado River valley, the people were given a choice of eggs that caused them to split into several groups. Those who chose brightly colored blue eggs continued toward the Middle Place but split into three groups. After numerous adventures, the main group founded a series of settlements in the Zuni river valley, eventually settling at *Halona Itiwana*, the Middle Place, now Zuni pueblo.

Research is ongoing to identify the places mentioned in the oral traditions, both the place of emergence and the various locations where the migrants paused and founded villages, also areas of symbolic and ritual importance. But can one take these historical accounts unduly literally? As Zuni interpreters of the oral traditions point out, the routes mentioned in chants and prayers do not describe exact routes. They tell us that ancestors of the modern-day Zuni traveled over a wide area of the south-west, some of it outside the present homeland. The challenge for archaeologists, and for Zuni historians, is to reconcile different perspectives on the ancestors. Their precious oral traditions are as precious and are as finite and likely to vanish as the archaeology of their past.

We're now entering a new era when many more people understand that archaeology is far more than just excavation and survey. One can legitimately ask whether the finite archaeological records of the past will survive into future centuries. It is highly likely they will, but in a much-depleted state. Fortunately, there's a slowly increasing awareness that we define ourselves to a significant extent through our past. Without it, we exist in a meaningless vacuum. And filling much of that vacuum is what the archaeology of today, and of the future, is all about.

Figure 13. The power of the supernatural. The Pyramid of the Sun at Teotihuacán, Mexico, which its constructors believed covered a mystical pathway to the Otherworld.

8 Why Archaeology Matters

The past surrounds us on every side, offering guidance and precedents, warnings, and sometimes reassurance. We cannot, of course, use the past as a way of forecasting what will happen next. The collapse of ancient Maya civilization or of the Roman empire, to mention only two examples, yield no clues as to whether today's civilizations will implode or survive. Archaeology is not in the prophecy business, but it gives humanity a past—six million or so years of experience. The fleeting, intimate glimpses of ancient times show us that we share many behavioral traits with our diverse ancestors.

Archaeology, with its long-term perspective, reminds us that we *Homo sapiens* are all very closely related, and all the same species. Yet, despite our common physical and mental attributes, archaeology reveals infinite cultural expressions of what it means to be human. How people lived, and how they thought about things, varied wildly. In this sense, archaeology gives us a narrative that shows us the ways in which human diversity began and then flourished. It provides a framework, and some guidance, for understanding how humans behaved.

Despite providing profound insights into who we are, the relevance of archaeology in today's world has nonetheless been questioned in many quarters. We now live in an era where short attention spans and instant gratification are realities. Short-term thinking is required in rapidly changing societies, which means that long-term perspectives, and long-term planning, appear not to make sense. How can we plan for the long-term when everything is shifting under our feet? The answer, of course, is that we must, especially in the context of major challenges to humanity that lurk in the near-term and on the distant horizon. Some of these are much discussed: rising population densities, especially in cities, the swelling economic and social chasm between rich and poor, and, most prominently in the public eye, human-caused global warming and climate change.

On the other hand, we are still faced with those who manipulate and invent the past to support their own ends, who sometimes go so far as to forge artifacts to support their version of the past, or to claim long-time occupation of their region. This has precedence: we need only recall Gustaf Kossinna (Chapter 5), who famously peddled nationalistic ideas of German racial superiority and manipulated the past to argue for primordial German rights over vast territories. Throughout this small book we have witnessed how archaeology has the tools to examine and, if necessary, counter such claims, frequently offering us powerful weapons against bigotry.

For while our societies certainly varied over time and space, we *Homo sapiens* have the same cerebral and cultural potential. In other words, if a certain group "failed" to do something (for example settle down and farm), it was simply that their world order did not require it, rather than because they were mentally inferior (as was once widely assumed).

Archaeology repeatedly demonstrates our unity, if only by showing that each area of the world had many ways of doing things at different times. This is of great relevance to the future of our increasingly globalized world: after all, its economic and social success depends on us all coming together in work and life. Moreover, as evolutionary geneticist Mark Thomas has observed, it seems that population density and migratory activity have always driven our cultural and economic explosions, rather than brain biology per se—if anything, our brain size has been static over the past 120,000 years. In other words, interconnectivity is essential for sparking new ideas. Yet we now live in a world of bordered nation states, in which leaders wish to curtail movement and build walls to keep others out. The past tells us this is not the path to human innovation.

Other pressing worldwide issues, such as global warming or social inequality, are areas where archaeology is developing valuable perspectives into the ways ancient societies adapted to these problems, albeit on a smaller scale. What happened before is, of course, not a statement about what will happen in the future. But to claim that the remotest past is irrelevant to today's realities is, clearly, untrue.

Exploring Big Issues

Archaeology is working to support arguments and solutions for big, global issues, such as the ways in which humans have caused climate change. These days, no one, except committed ideologues, believes that climate shifts in our warming world are simply natural cycles, similar to those that have unfolded over millions of years. We live in a world that has ventured into uncharted climatic waters, where humans, with our fossil fuels and environmental disruptions, are the dominant agents. Thanks to the revolution in paleoclimatology, we now know a great deal about climatic shifts since the end of the Ice Age 12,000 years ago, and more every day about the climatic background to human existence over the past three million years.

A large number of archaeologists are now assessing the impacts of long- and short-term climatic change on human societies ranging from small bands to entire pre-industrial cities. As the pace of research accelerates, we're acquiring a much more sophisticated understanding of climate as a major player in such past developments as the first settlement of the Americas, the origins of agriculture, and the beginnings of civilization. Above all, we're acquiring insights into how different societies adapted to drought cycles, sea level rises, and such events as El Niños, and the various economic, political, and social consequences of climate change. We've discovered, for example, just how important ties of kin and links between ancient small-scale societies, even city neighborhoods, could be when hurricanes descend or flooding menaces farming villages. The same ties, often overlooked, are powerful tools for those surviving the major disasters of today, especially in poverty-stricken areas—and in an era of more frequent extreme weather events. Today's multidisciplinary, team-based archaeology is a weapon in the debates about climate change, past and future.

There is also the issue of social inequality. It has a long legacy: the first pre-industrial civilizations appeared around 5,000 years ago. All of them depended on strongly centralized economic, political, and social organization, where the commoners labored to support a much smaller number of nobles, high officials, priests, and, at the pinnacle, a ruler who was often careful to claim some form of connection with the gods. Thousands of anonymous workers and vast amounts of animal power sustained them. In contemporary parlance, these were societies with haves and have-nots, no different to those in industrialized societies today.

Social inequality has been part of human society for a very long time and comes in many guises. Chiefs and monarchies cemented their power by cultivating kin ties and loyalty. Pharaohs ruled because of the precedent of perceived divine authority. Power and wealth have always gone together, and archaeology offers a unique perspective into how power relationships arise and change through time.

Social and economic inequality is a topic that is of great interest to archaeologists. In Roman times, for example, the gap between rich and poor was enormous. Society was so stratified that the top 2 percent or so of the populace absorbed almost all available surpluses beyond those essential for basic subsistence. Social inequality is as old as civilization, especially in societies that promoted ideologies of divine rulership—for example the demigod Roman emperors, or the semi-divine pharaohs of Egypt, whose authority was that of the gods, so *had* to be followed.

The degree of stratification varied from one civilization to another. Unfortunately, studying ancient inequality is very challenging, even with the increasingly vast data sets that archaeologists are gathering. Conventionally, grave furniture has been used as a measure of wealth, which is obvious enough if you contemplate the tomb of Tutankhamun or a Lord of Sipán and compare them to the unadorned graves of commoners. Bone health reflects nutrition; pathological conditions are barometers of years of harsh labor; but measuring degrees of social inequality requires more subtle indicators.

Working in southwestern Colorado, Tim Kohler and others are using a measure of economic inequality developed by an Italian statistician, Corrado Gini, as long ago as 1912. The Gini coefficient is used widely today to measure differences in the levels of health between members of society. It uses economic data provided by modern governments. Ancient societies have no such data, so various proxies have been employed, among them the size of fields; but the most widely applicable measure seems to be relative house size.

Kohler and his colleagues have examined data from sixty-three locales across North and Central America, as well as Eurasia, calling on local experts for assistance with the variables. They've found greater wealth disparities in the Old World than the Americas; perhaps, they theorize, because of the larger domesticated animals in the former, which multiplied the impacts of human labor. The research continues, but it's a fascinating example of the kind of insights that are emerging from research into the past that have relevance in our debates on inequality today.

Writing Unwritten History

As witnessed throughout this book, while archaeology tends to be a product of small trenches and specialized research, its results are enormously important to humankind: it alone puts us in touch with our global past. This may seem a remarkable statement, but it is true. Much more than was once realized, the multidisciplinary archaeology of today has written vast chapters of history for societies all over the world, whose past was previously unwritten. With trowels, spades, radar, and more, it is recovering much of early sub-Saharan African history, developing and exploring new chapters of Chinese history, and helping with the story of the colonization of Polynesia. Most importantly of all, it peers into a past that is not all statesmen and generals, palaces and royal achievements. It also gives us all a past that predates writing. In countries such as the UK, this means anything before the Romans—a mere drop in the ocean of time for archaeology. Meanwhile, for those settled in countries with no pre-colonial written history, it gives, at least in general terms, an historical identity.

We tend to think of the past in simplistic terms, which means that we assume that more recent societies were much less socially diverse than they were. Ancient Rome was a remarkably cosmopolitan city. So were Teotihuacán (see Figure 13) and the Aztec Tenochtitlán in pre-Columbian highland Central America. Here, again, archaeology excels, for our excavations yield a great deal of the commonplace and anonymous—the artifacts of slaves' quarters in Colonial America, Chinese laborers' encampments in the Higher Sierra, California, earthquake victims in a Roman town in Cyprus. Like the harshly treated laborers at pharaoh Akhenaten's capital by the Nile, they lived their lives in anonymity. Their only voices are their bodies, their artifacts, and sometimes whispers of the intangible in ritual objects and oral traditions. And yet, despite this unique source of information about ourselves, we're looting and destroying the very fabric of our history.

The Future of the Past

Archaeology is a guardian of the past, and still works hard to ensure it does so for the benefit of everyone. One of its greatest enemies is the illegal trade in antiquities, which is, and always has been, vandalism of humanity's shared cultural heritage. Not only does looting take many priceless finds away from public view, it also destroys the context of the objects, which could have been recovered by careful, systematic excavation and analysis. A looted find such as a marble statue of a Cycladic harpist (see Figure 14) or a Maya painted pot taken from a noble's grave becomes a mere art object displayed behind glass in a museum or on a shelf at home. It no longer tells the historical story that was once an integral part of its being.

How does one fight this pernicious vandalism, called eloquently "a scourge of historical knowledge, local pride, and international sovereignty" by Evangelos Kyriakidis on online news site The Conversation. Part of the fight is to promulgate the ethical standards by which we approach the past. Archaeologists have done a good job of laying out ethical boundaries for themselves, many of which have direct relevance to the public at large.

So where is archaeology going to go next? Achieving much closer understanding of human cultures, in all their diversity, over the long span of the past is, and will remain, its major concern. Archaeology's increasingly sophisticated research, much of it involving non-intrusive fieldwork, are also more and more significant. Thanks in part to a heavy involvement in science and in multidisciplinary research, we've journeyed a long way from the solitary excavations of yesteryear, and even further from the tomb-raiding and gun-toting adventures stereotyped by Hollywood.

It is quite likely that archaeology's priorities are about to change profoundly as it redoubles its focus on conservation. As the American archaeologist Kent Flannery once joked, "Archaeology is the only social science where we kill our informants to study them." The archaeological record is a finite resource and, in excavating, we destroy it. A variety of awe-inspiring scientific innovations, however, mean that excavation is no longer always necessary, nor even always preferable. All this is heralding a seismic change in the discipline. These kinds of non-intrusive, as well as laboratory, research currently involve everything from genetic and isotope analysis to LiDAR survey. They are something that everyone in archaeology, whether culture heritage specialists, government officials, or academics, will have to draw upon.

Figure 14. A Cycladic harpist from the Grove of Keros, Keros Island, Aegean Sea. Such stylized figurines date to around 2500 BC and are known mainly from graves of both men and women. Their significance is unknown.

While a good portion of archaeological work will still be driven by university research and cultural resource management (developer-funded work), there will also likely be far greater global emphasis on heritage management and tourism, public archaeology, and stakeholders, with all the conservation and outreach activities that this implies. This begins with the politics and values of today's archaeology.

Until recently, conservation and heritage were somewhat in the background. Tourist counts at archaeological sites or the impact of visiting crowds were issues out of the limelight. The old desire for original discovery masked the vital importance of preserving our heritage for future generations, and of curbing vandalism. The next half century will witness the shift of archaeology toward a profession devoted to preserving the past, and presenting it for everyone. One likes to assume that the most lauded archaeologists of future generations will be those who devote their careers to working on these concerns. The issues of deep history will still be important, as they should be, but the major thrust of archaeology will be at the local level, with communities and their stakeholders, in attempts to preserve what is left and to make people aware of how precious our heritage remains.

The challenges are enormous, given the rapid expansion of cultural tourism, and the social pressures that bear on any studies of human diversity, whether ancient or modern. Viking Jorvik, the medieval town that is now a major heritage attraction in York, England, has long involved local people in its work. In Ireland, St. Kevin founded an early monastic settlement at Glendalough in County Wicklow, in the sixth century AD. Glendalough, with its distinctive circular tower, which still stands, flourished despite Viking attacks and became a major center of learning until the Normans destroyed the monastery in 1214. An archaeological project around the monastery complex involving local community members has revealed many features, including a ditched enclosure. Community archaeology projects are proliferating across the world, investigating convict houses in Australia, Malay quarters in Cape Town, South Africa, and neighborhoods in Alexandria, Virginia, USA.

So who is tomorrow's archaeologist? In an ideal world, he or she will have a very broad training. This will begin with a solid academic grounding that reflects not only the basic method and theory of archaeology, but also a strong multidisciplinary perspective, which is where research archaeology has long been headed. Future archaeologists will need a firm grasp of the practicalities of cultural resource management and the fundamental skills needed for that kind of work, including rigorous training in public speaking and general, not only academic, writing skills. Finally, their training should include in-depth exposure to working with stakeholders, and a grounding in conservation and cultural heritage. This is a formidable list, to be sure, which could be addressed by some more specialized branching within MA or even PhD programs, but it should be remembered that the real issue with much of archaeology is not pure research but dealing with how archaeology intersects and contributes to the wider world: practical, day-to-day issues that are encountered with conservation, CRM, public outreach, and heritage/tourism activities. There is also a growing demand for highly trained technicians, whose entire careers will be devoted to specialist inquiries, and to background research for all kinds of arcane issues, from conservation of mud bricks to protecting rock art or dissecting the details of burials in

Figure 15. Monk's Mound, Cahokia, Illinois, built between AD 1050 and 1200. This is the largest ancient earthwork in North America.

a mass sepulcher. Such experts will be in the background of tomorrow's archaeology, as much part of teams working on the past as top-level academic specialists.

Why It Matters

Does archaeology matter in today's industrialized world? Surely it matters more than ever. We are achieving understandings of ancient human behavior, and of our biological and cultural diversity, which were unimaginable a few decades ago. Above all, archaeologists are stewards of the magnificent cultural heritage of humanity. Our job is to present the past as accessible and as something we all have a share in, whether an earthwork in the Midwest of the United States (see Figure 15), fragments of an ancient Maori canoe from New Zealand, or the megaliths at Stonehenge in southern England. There's much to be done, but we're slowly moving in the right direction, but probably not urgently enough.

If we lose this priceless heritage to greed and vandalism, warfare and industrial activity, or promiscuous construction, we lose our credibility as thinking human beings. We owe the past not only to ourselves and to still unborn generations, but also to those who created it. To quote Søren Kierkegaard, the great nineteenth-century Danish philosopher: "Life can only be understood backwards; but it must be lived forwards." Certainly, to know ourselves fully, we have to understand our past. And, regardless of the mind-boggling cultural diversity that we find across time and space, as paleontologist Stephen Jay Gould remarked, we all come from the same human twig. Archaeology celebrates this reality, which is why it matters.

Further Reading

Bulging library shelves and numerous popular and academic journals tell the story of the past. Navigation through these confusing literary waters is rapidly becoming a near impossibility for the general reader. The annotated commentary that follows offers a sampling of books that we've found useful as starting points. Each contains a comprehensive bibliography, which will lead you to other sources. We do not list papers or websites here (with one exception) and would point out that a great deal of the material below is not widely published.

1 Revealing Deep History

Deetz, James, *Invitation to Archaeology* (Garden City, NY: Natural History Press, 1967).

This brief paperback is a classic statement on how archaeology works, written in lyrical prose.

Fagan, Brian, *A Little History of Archaeology* (London and New Haven: Yale University Press, 2017).

A punchy history written in short chapters that describes the work of major archaeologists and what they learned about the past.

Fagan, Brian and Durrani, Nadia, *People of the Earth*, 15th edition (Abingdon: Routledge, 2019).

A survey of world prehistory aimed at undergraduates.

Kelly, Robert L., *The Fifth Beginning: What Six Million Years of History Can Tell Us About Our Future* (Berkeley: University of California Press, 2016).

Kelly's masterly essay, written with a delightful sense of humor and in an occasionally folksy style, examines the issues of the past and the future.

Sabloff, Jeremy A., *Archaeology Matters: Action Anthropology in the Modern World* (Abingdon: Routledge, 2008).

A carefully argued, elegant survey of archaeology's importance and the need for archaeology to be involved in society.

Scarre, Chris (ed.), *The Human Past* (London and New York: Thames and Hudson, 2018).

A comprehensive survey of human prehistory, written by leading experts for more advanced students.

2 Investigating Climate Change

Campbell, Bruce, *The Great Transition: Climate, Disease and Society in the Late-Medieval World* (Cambridge: Cambridge University Press, 2016).

Described by one reviewer as a "bible," this is a comprehensive introduction to a complex subject.

Fagan, Brian, *Chaco Canyon: Archaeologists Explore the Lives of an Ancient Society* (New York: Oxford University Press, 2005).

Chaco defies easy interpretation. Fagan's general account for a broad audience summarizes the major sites and issues.

Fagan, Brian, *Floods, Famines, and Emperors: El Niño and the Fate of Civilizations*, rev. edition (New York: Basic Books, 2009).

Somewhat outdated, this is a general account of the history of El Niños for a wide audience.

Gaffney, Vincent, et al., *Europe's Lost World: The Rediscovery of Doggerland* (York: Council for British Archaeology, 2009).

Describes the remote sensing and other research that went into the reconstruction of the now-sunken land below the North Sea.

Harper, Kyle, *The Fate of Rome: Climate, Disease, and the End of an Empire* (Princeton, NJ: Princeton University Press, 2017).

No book does a better job of assessing the impact of climate change (and indeed plague) on an ancient civilization than this brilliant study.

Lieberman, Benjamin and Gordon, Elizabeth, *Climate Change in Human History: Prehistory to the Present* (New York: Bloomsbury Academic, 2018).

Useful for its bibliography, this is an undergraduate textbook that offers a broad, fast-moving survey.

Vivian, R. Gwinn and Hilpert, Bruce, *Chaco Handbook: An Encyclopedia Guide*, 2nd edition (Salt Lake City: University of Utah Press, 2012).

Everything you want to know about Chaco and more in a comprehensive synthesis.

Webster, David L., *The Fall of the Ancient Maya: Solving the Mystery of the Maya Collapse* (London: Thames and Hudson, 2002).

Webster's authoritative and broad-based survey of the collapse is an admirable guide to a complex subject by an established expert.

3 Revealing Who We Are

Gall, Michael J. and Veit, Richard F. (eds.), *Archaeologies of African-American Life in the Upper Mid-Atlantic*, 2nd edition (Tuscaloosa: University of Alabama Press, 2017).

Contains a valuable series of case studies that provide essential background. A useful starting point.

Hoffecker, John, *Modern Humans: Their African Origin and Global Dispersal* (New York: Columbia University Press, 2017).

Up-to-date and wide-ranging, this is the most comprehensive account available for general readers.

Liebmann, Matthew, *Revolt: An Archaeological History of Pueblo Resistance and Revitalization in 17th Century New Mexico* (Tucson: University of Arizona Press, 2012).

The Pueblo Revolt approached from a multidisciplinary perspective, working closely with the Jemez people. An exemplary account of contemporary research.

Manco, Jean, *Ancestral Journeys: The Peopling of Europe from the First Venturers to the Vikings* (London and New York: Thames and Hudson, 2013).

Shows the potential of genetics in studying the more remote, and more recent, human past.

Reich, David, *Who We Are and How We Got Here: Ancient DNA and the New Science of the Human Past* (New York: Oxford University Press, 2018).

An authoritative and wide-ranging account of genetics and the human past for a general audience.

Samford, Patricia, *Subfloor Pits and the Archaeology of Slavery in Virginia* (Tuscaloosa: University of Alabama Press, 2007).

Samford's fascinating study of slave quarters between the seventeenth and mid-nineteenth centuries examines not only lifeways, but also traditional beliefs and resistance.

Spindler, Konrad, *The Man in the Ice* (New York: Harmony Books, 1995).

Spindler's account of the discovery of the Iceman, although somewhat outdated by more recent bioanthropological studies, is still an informative read.

Wolf, Eric, *Europe and the People Without History* (Berkeley: University of California Press, 1982).

Wolf's closely argued book, which revolves around the European Age of Discovery, is a major source on people without documented pasts.

4 Exploring Gender

Galle, J. E. and Young, A. L. (eds.), *Engendering African-American Archaeology: A Southern Perspective* (Knoxville: University of Tennessee Press, 2004).

Opens up a neglected field of gender research with good examples.

Gero, J. M. and Conkey, M. W. (eds.) *Engendering Archaeology* (Oxford: Blackwell, 1991).

A fundamental, pioneering source that is still of value.

Hastorf, C., *Agriculture and the Onset of Political Inequality before the Inka* (Cambridge: Cambridge University Press, 1992).

Exemplary research on the Sausa with a focus on gender.

Joyce, Rosemary A., *Ancient Bodies, Ancient Lives* (London: Thames and Hudson, 2008).

A brilliant and indispensable essay on gender and sexual identity, which serves as an authoritative and thought-provoking starting point.

Nelson, Sarah Milledge (ed.) *Handbook of Gender in Archaeology* (Lanham, MD: Rowman and Littlefield, 2006).

A wide-ranging set of essays on gender, drawing from many parts of the world to form a provocative and interesting source book.

Rotman, Deborah L., *The Archaeology of Gender in Historic America* (Gainesville: University of Florida Press, 2015).

An up-to-date synthesis of gender and materiality in historic North America. Has an interesting emphasis on the role of food.

Spector, Janet, *What This Awl Means: Feminist Archaeology at a Wahpeton Dakota Village* (Minneapolis: Minnesota Historical Society, 1993).

A classic essay on a woman's awl, which is a wonderful introduction to the challenges of gender research.

5 Archaeology and Nationalism

Boytner, Ran, Swartz, Lynn, and Parker, Bradley J. (eds.), *Controlling the Past, Owning the Future: The Political Uses of Archaeology in the Middle East* (Tucson: University of Arizona Press, 2010).

The contributors examine the political uses and misuses of archaeology in the Middle Eastern and eastern Mediterranean world, including the consequences of their own work.

Card, Jeb J. and Anderson, David S. (eds.), *Lost City, Lost Pyramid: Understanding Alternative Archaeologies and Pseudoscientific Practices* (Tuscaloosa: University of Alabama Press, 2016).

An edited volume of twelve perceptive essays on pseudo-archaeology that is strong on case studies.

Crossrail, *Tunnel: The Archaeology of Crossrail* (London: Crossrail, 2017). [Available through the Museum of London]

A popular account of the fascinating discoveries made by the Crossrail Project for a general audience. Lavishly illustrated.

Diaz-Andreu, Margarita and Champion, Timothy (eds.), *Nationalism and Archaeology in Europe* (Abingdon: Routledge, 2014).

Archaeologists from throughout Europe explore the relationship between nationalistic ideas and archaeology during the nineteenth and twentieth centuries.

Feder, Kenneth, *Frauds, Myths, and Mysteries: Science and Pseudoscience in Archaeology*, 9th edition (New York: Oxford University Press, 2017).

Feder's well-written and engaging textbook on the subject is an invaluable source on the zany side of archaeology.

Roesdahl, Else, *The Vikings*, 3rd edition, trans. Susan M. Margeson and Kirsten Williams (New York: Penguin, 1991).

An encyclopedic synthesis of the Vikings and the Viking Age that paints a broad-brushed portrait of the Norse and their impact on history.

Silverberg, Robert, *The Moundbuilders of Ancient America* (New York: New York Graphic Society, 1968).

The Moundbuilders is a fundamental source on this enduring controversy.

6 The Tourist Effect

Cronyn, J. M., *Elements of Archaeological Conservation* (Abingdon: Routledge, 1990).

Cronyn's admirable summary is based on years of practical and pedagogical experience. It has been around for a while, but is first rate.

McManamon, Francis P. (ed.), *New Perspectives in Cultural Resource Management* (Abingdon: Routledge, 2017).

The contributors to this important book have vast CRM experience and look both at current activity and at the shape of CRM in the future.

Messenger, Phyllis Mauch and Smith, George S. (eds.), *Cultural Heritage Management: A Global Perspective* (Gainesville: University Press of Florida, 2014).

Messenger's and Smith's edited volume is a useful introduction to cultural heritage from a global perspective.

Timothy, Dallen J., *Cultural Heritage and Tourism: An Introduction* (Bristol, UK: Channel View Publications, 2011).

The author is passionate about cultural heritage and it shows in this wide-ranging introduction to a complex subject.

7 Protecting the Past

Alva, Walter and Donnan, Christopher, *Royal Tombs of Sipán* (Los Angeles: Fowler Museum of Cultural History, 1989).

A lavishly illustrated, popular account of the Moche warrior priests in all their funerary glory. This is a triumph of writing on conservation and preservation.

Brodie, Neil and Walker Tubb, Kathryn, *Illicit Antiquities: The Theft of Culture and the Extinction of Archaeology* (Abingdon: Routledge, 2001).

Mackenzie, Simon et al., *Trafficking Culture: Transnational Criminal Markets and the Illicit Trade in Cultural Objects* (Abingdon: Routledge, 2018).

The above two books present a sobering assessment of the dangers facing archaeology from the international antiquities trade and of the legal challenges in combatting it. Both should be compulsory reading for archaeologists and others.

Budge, Wallis, *By Nile and Tigris* (London: John Murray, 1920).

Pompous, self-serving, and at times downright dishonest, Wallis Budge's account of his adventures in Egypt and Mesopotamia is a primer of late nineteenth-century plundering for museums. It is listed here purely as an example!

Colwell, Chip, *Plundered Skulls and Stolen Spirits: Inside the Fight to Reclaim Native America's Culture* (Chicago: University of Chicago Press, 2017).

Colwell is a curator with an inside view of the complexities of repatriating skeletal remains and NAGPRA. He discusses complex issues surrounding the ownership of the past.

Mayer, Karl E., *The Plundered Past: The Story of the Illegal International Traffic in Works of Art* (New York: Macmillan, 1977).

Karl Meyer's pioneering essay on the ravaging of the past is a minor classic. Readable, entertaining, and direct, it can be strongly recommended as a starting point.

Meskell, Lynn, *A Future in Ruins: UNESCO, World Heritage, and the Dream of Peace* (New York: Oxford University Press, 2018).

Meskell's provocative and hard-hitting book is a must-read for anyone concerned about cultural heritage and tourism. It tackles the issue of Euro-centrism and nationalism head on.

Watkins, Joe, *Indigenous Archaeology: American Indian Values and Scientific Practice* (Lanham, MD: AltaMira Press, 2013).

Lays out the fundamental principles behind indigenous archaeology in the context of Native America. American archaeology is changing and this study records some of the figures for a sobering assessment.

8 Why Archaeology Matters

Many of the topics mentioned in this chapter are covered in references to earlier ones, so there is little to add.

Burtenshaw, Paul, *Archaeology and Economic Development* (Abingdon: Routledge, 2017).

A thought-provoking discussion of archaeology's engagement with economic development.

Kohler, Timothy and Smith, Michel E. (eds.), *Ten Thousand Years of Inequality: The Archaeology of Wealth Differences* (Tucson: University of Arizona Press, 2018).

The numerous contributors to this edited volume bring together studies of social inequality through history for the first time. An important foundation for future research.

Little, Barbara J. (ed.), *Public Benefits of Archaeology* (Gainesville: University of Florida Press, 2002).

An eclectic and invaluable collection of papers on why archaeology matters beyond research. Some papers are by non-archaeologists.

Moshenka, Gabriel (ed.), *Key Concepts in Public Archaeology* (London: UCL Press, 2017).

Essays on public archaeology with a British slant.

Zeder, Melinda, *The American Archaeologist: A Profile* (Walnut Creek, CA: AltaMira Press, 1997).

An important study of a changing American archaeology, which details major trends, now accelerating.

Picture Credits

Figure 1: Juan Aunion/Alamy Stock Photo
Figure 2: Alexander Maleev
Figure 3: Chris Selby/age fotostock/SuperStock
Figure 4: Robert Harding/SuperStock
Figure 5: The Metropolitan Museum of Art, New York, Acc. No. 33.8.16, Rogers Fund, 1933
Figure 6: National Geographic Image Collection/Bridgeman Images
Figure 7: De Agostini/SuperStock
Figure 8: Heritage Image Partnership/Alamy Stock Photo
Figure 9: Christine Mariner/Design Pics/SuperStock
Figure 10: Tom Bean/Alamy Stock Photo
Figure 11: Valery Sharifulin/ITAR-TASS News Agency/Alamy Stock Photo
Figure 12: Christopher Furlong /Getty Images
Figure 13: Steve Vidler/SuperStock
Figure 14: The Metropolitan Museum of Art, New York, Acc. No. 47.100.1, Rogers Fund, 1947
Figure 15: Carver Mostardi/Alamy Stock Photo

Plate 1: WaterFrame/Alamy Stock Photo
Plate 2: Universal Images Group North America LLC/DeAgostini/ Alamy Stock Photo
Plate 3: The Metropolitan Museum of Art, New York, Acc. No. 64.228.21, Gift of Mr. and Mrs. Nathan Cummings, 1964
Plate 4: Werner Forman Archive/Heritage Image Partnership Ltd/ Alamy Stock Photo
Plate 5: Martin Thomas Photography/Alamy Stock Photo
Plate 6: Rapp Halour/Alamy Stock Photo
Plate 7: Prisma/Album/SuperStock
Plate 8: Robert Harding/SuperStock
Plate 9: Justin Tallis/AFP/Getty Images
Plate 10: Westend61/SuperStock
Plate 11: Dereje Belachew/Alamy Stock Photo
Plate 12: John Henshall/Alamy Stock Photo
Plate 13: Lena Kuhnt/age fotostock/SuperStock
Plate 14: Rose Araya-Farias/Heritage Image Partnership Ltd/ Alamy Stock Photo
Plate 15: Frans Lemmens/Alamy Stock Photo
Plate 16: Lambros Kazanas/Alamy Stock Photo

Index